658.85 C357t   1/23/04
Catal, Joe.
Telesales tips from the
trenches   JAN 2 3 2004

Telesales Tips FROM THE Trenches

SECRETS OF A STREET-SMART SALESMAN

JOE CATAL aka "Sale-Man"

WITHDRAWN

Business By Phone Inc.

13254 Stevens St., Omaha, NE 68137   402-895-9
www.businessbyphone.com

Telesales Tips from the Trenches
By Joe Catal

Copyright 2002, Business By Phone Inc.
All rights reserved

Reproduction of any portion of this book for individual use is permitted if credit is given to Joe Catal, author, and Business By Phone Inc., publisher. Any systematic or multiple reproduction (photocopies) or distribution by any means, including electronic, of any part of this book, or inclusion in publications is permitted by permission only.

Published By:

Business By Phone Inc.
13254 Stevens St.
Omaha, NE 68137.
(402)895-9399
Fax:(402)896-3353
E-mail telesales@businessbyphone.com
www.BusinessByPhone.com

Cover design by George Foster, Foster & Foster, Fairfield, IA

ISBN 1-881081-15-x

My Personal Thanks to Art Sobczak

I met Art Sobczak, President of Business By Phone (publisher of this book) several years ago at one of his telesales seminars. At that time I was reading his *"Telephone Selling Report"* newsletter. I always liked his ideas and concepts, and wanted to learn as much as I could from this man. I've attended many seminars on sales, but Art's simply blew me away. I was already doing well, but he showed me how the sales process worked.

I personally believe Art is the best in the business. I look up to him as my mentor, and have watched his own company grow and keep up with the times. His Ideas and concepts are for the real world of selling. I personally want to thank him, along with my family for the opportunity to not only better myself, but also help others. The most important thing I've learned from Art over the years is not just how to make great money, but how important it is to help other people grow and be a better person. He's the reason this book was written.

Thanks for giving me the tools and knowledge to become a better person. You're the best Art.

Joe Catal

AKA "Sale-Man"

Contents

10. Presentation Ideas *(continued)*

Presentation Ideas *(continued)*

11. Exercises to Help Plan Your Calls 60

12. Dealing With Mid-Level Managers 63

13. Closing Strategies and Techniques 66

13. Closing Strategies and Techniques *(continued)*

14. Last Resort Closing Techniques 81

14. Last Resort Closing Techniques *(continued)*

15. The Price Issue 84

16. Asking for Referrals 94

20. Prospecting Tips *(continued)*

Introduction

Hi. My name's Joe Catal. This book has hundreds upon hundreds of ideas and concepts you can incorporate immediately to increase sales and avoid rejection.

This book is the result of my research and experience, and you'll be a beneficiary. These techniques are tested.

I've been a phone sales street fighter since 1985. Like you, I'm in the trenches every day banging out 50-100 calls a day. I'm constantly testing, tweaking, and refining techniques. Some with great success, some not. Every day, week in and week out I hear my share of no's just like you. But what sticks in my mind the most are the thousand or so yes's representing millions of dollars worth of sales.

I have a lot of real-life experience (some call it the "school of hard knocks"), but you'll never live long enough to experience everything yourself that you would need to become a master. That's why I'm a sales information junkie. I've been to numerous seminars, read hundreds of books and newsletters, and listened to thousands of hours of tapes about sales and marketing strategies. No matter how the information is put out, I find it. What this means to you, fellow sales pro, is that you're getting the best ideas and concepts that are my own, after I've gleaned tips, ideas, methods, processes and theories by many other authors.

Believe me, there's lots of sales garbage out there. I've cut through the crap, tested what looked like had a chance, and now I'm sharing the best, most successful ideas with you.

The best way to use this book is to read through it first, and hi-lite the ideas that jump right out at you.

You should also highlight any authors I cite. You'd be amazed at the creative ideas and systems people use to get an edge over you.

This book is written for the person who's picking up a phone and calling someone they don't know ... when the prospect has never heard of you, and you don't have a recognizable company name, yet you need to set an appointment, or ask them for money right then and there.

If you're fortunate enough to work for a company that does mail outs, a substantial marketing budget, or has a recognizable name, so much the better. But for most of us who have to bang out 50-100 calls a day to a total stranger to get a pay check, you'll love this book.

There's no theory or hype in this book. What you read today, you can apply today. This book will teach you streetsmart and booksmart skills. Too much street talk without knowledge of selling process is useless. Too much book theory and not enough street smarts makes you lose sales because you can't let go and just be yourself. You need to incorporate a bit of both.

This book is a blend of soft sell and hard sell strategies. If you're too soft you lose sales. Too hard, and it turns people off. This book will be a fun and interesting read for you. Incorporate what applies to you, and toss out what doesn't. It's really that simple. We'll start out with basic fundamentals you need to succeed as an individual or a company, and progressively get more in depth. Now let's get started.

KNOWLEDGE + ACTION =SUCCESS

Joe Catal

a.k.a. *Sale-Man*

1

Are you Losing Money When You Answer Your Phones?

Before I get started showing you how to make money on the phone, you first have to know how to use it. If you're a business owner or manager, you better pay close attention because your company is more than likely losing about 20% in annual sales.

Does your company have a specific training program written out on how to answer the phone and take proper messages?

Don't just assume because someone has years of experience they know how to answer a phone. Is everyone in the company answering the phone the same way?

Are people in your office saying stupid things like:

"He's out to lunch."

"I don't know where he is."

"He's not in, call back later."

"Can you hold a minute while I get a pen?"

"He's in the bathroom."

"I don't know when he'll be back."

"Do you want to leave a message?"

The list goes on, but you get the point. If you or your people are saying these things, you're losing money.

Here's how to fix the problem. First of all, everyone needs to answer the phone the same way. Here are a couple of ways to choose from. Make sure ALL of your employees including yourself use one of these methods.

> **"Hello, ABC Services, Joe speaking. How may I help you today?"**

> **"Hello, ABC Services, Joe speaking. How may I assist you today?"**

You'd be amazed how many people answer the phone, with *"Hello?"* or *"Yeah?"* and not even mention the company name.

A lot of people like to answer the phone with, *"It's a great day at ABC Service."* That's lame! The person's voice doesn't project that it is a great day. They're just saying it, and it gives the company a fake image. If you want to say something like that, here's how:

> **"Hello, ABC Service, Joe speaking. How can I give you great customer service today?"**

Now that's a show stopper! This does several things. First, it usually stops people in their tracks and they typically make a positive comment. Second, it immediately puts your employee in a *responsibility mode.* This is key. It's letting people know you will personally give good customer service. I suggest you let your employees choose the statement that best suits them.

People like doing business with a company that has all its people on the same page. You need to incorporate this right away.

Transferring Calls

Another problem I've found is that 20-30% of the people who answer the phone don't know how to properly transfer people to voice mail. I hear things like, "I don't know how to use it. I don't know if we have that," etc. Make sure anyone who answers the phone knows how to use it. It makes your employees come off as stupid if they don't. It makes people think they must not be too smart over there. Also make sure they ask the person if they would like to be transferred into voice mail. People hate it when they call a business and ask for someone only to be put into their voice mail. Don't tell people so and so's out to lunch. If someone's not in, tell them they're on an outside appointment and that you'd be more than happy to take a message. If you're leaving the office, make sure people know what time you'll be back.

Don't ask people if they want to leave a message—just take the message!

You'll get sales you'd otherwise miss. That's because people who are shopping around don't call back. If the person they want isn't in, you should say,

"Jim will be back between two and three. What number can he reach you at? How do you spell your last name? What time will you be available for him to call?"

As you can see, you have to be proactive. You have to teach the people who answer your phone how to be a bit like a salesperson. Have them ask what the call is about. Have them ask the person if someone else can help them. Give customers options.

"Call Back Later"

"You'll have to call back later, all our technicians are at lunch."

What type of garbage is that!

You tell people how great your customer service is, now show them. There should always be a service rep on the premises. Have your reps take lunch at different times. If that's not possible, they should have cell phones so people can contact them. At the very least, tell the person you'll put a call into one of the service reps and they'll get back to you shortly. 90% of people don't change vendors because of price, they change because of poor service.

Key Point
Your customers are somebody else's prospects. If you won't take care of them, someone else will. (That's a guarantee.)

These are just basics of presenting a great image to your customers. Always remember, the first person to answer the phone is the person who sets the image for your company. You had better make sure they're professionally trained. If not, 20 to 30% of new business calling in is being lost.

Also, make sure the people answering your phones have a great voice. In the real world of business, if someone answers your phone who can't speak proper English, you're dead in the water. I'm not being prejudiced here, but I personally refuse to do business with anyone who can't understand English. If, for example, you work predominantly in the Spanish market, then you should have an English/Spanish-speaking person answering the phone. If your receptionist only speaks Spanish, you'll miss opportunities to expand.

Avoid Personal Calls

If your company has customers coming to your place of business, make sure they don't hear employees making personal calls. Who wants to hear about the fight you had with your boyfriend or girlfriend last night?

Never use vulgarity in front of customers. Anytime a customer is in your office or waiting room, the only thing they should hear or see is people working. Don't have a customer stand around for service while employees are on the phone talking to friends. You don't realize how much damage an employee can do to the image of your company. One negative comment, one vulgar word, an argument a customer hears, can be very costly to you.

Make sure that when someone calls you to get information on your offer, you then ask for the order! Don't just answer their questions and send them an info package.

Key Point

Anytime someone has interest in what you are offering, ask for an order. Always!

If your receptionist answers the phone, make sure she doesn't say, *"Ok, we'll send you something out. What's your address?"* You'll lose a ton of business that way. Have her transfer the person to a sales rep. Sell, sell, sell! Close, close, close! Have aggressive people on your phone.

Now lets start making money!

2

Time Management And Organization

Understand the difference between being efficient and being effective. It's the difference between doing something right and doing the right thing. Always focus on being effective!

Don't confuse activity with productivity. If you're doing paperwork during peak call times, you're not being productive. For the next week keep a log of your work habits. Here's an example.

If work starts at 9:00, are you ready to dial or did you get in at 9:20? Do you spend another 10 minutes going through your voice mail messages? Do you then spend another 20 minutes e-mailing everyone back (including friends who sent you attachments you have to see)? By that time it's 10:00, and you haven't even made a single call yet! Sure you were *busy*, but you weren't productive or effective. That's five hours of time lost a week, twenty hours a month! That means you're starting the month off minus 20 hours.

Time management studies have shown over and over that the average person who works eight hours a day spends less than three hours a day on their main activity. That means five hours a day is spent on non-productive activities. Think about that for a minute. That means in a 40-hour work week you worked only 15 hours on your main activity (dialing). As I said earlier, you need to spend 45 minutes of every working hour being productive (on the phone!). Poor time management is the number one reason why people have stress on their jobs. They simply can't prioritize the difference between activity and productivity. It's always something else with these people. I had to take these calls...I had to do this...you're always slowing me down...get out of my way, etc.

What they fail to realize is that 80% of their work habits

5

are spent on non-productive activities. Sure they're busy, but they're not getting their priority duties accomplished. That means everyone in that department or company is suffering. Don't let other people's poor time management take money out of your pocket. Set the example of what REAL WORK is. Stay on the phone all day, (45 minutes out of every hour). Let people know you're there to make money, not gab and play games. If you have a shipping department that's always running a day or two behind, and you have to constantly call customers to apologize, you can almost bet it's due to their poor time management. Don't put off your main job function for other activities that aren't productive. You can read the mail at lunch time or at the end of the day, not during peak call hours. Set dentist and other appointments during lunch hour or after work, not during your productive time.

Polish Your People Skills

You'll find that if a person has poor time management, they generally have bad people skills. They're always pointing the finger, explaining how their way is better, and how you're wrong. What they fail to realize is that they're the reason why the other parts of the company aren't functioning at 100% efficiency. Another trait about these people is that they're always making rules. Every day it's some new rule they think will help them work more efficiently. They keep telling employees the same things over and over but no one's listening. They simply don't have the respect of the employees because of their poor time management. Whenever they're on the phone with someone, you always hear them yelling at the person on the other end, "I want to talk to your supervisor!" These people haven't got a clue about time management or managing. If you're getting calls from customers on a regular basis on why their shipment's running late, or why things are taking so long, have the person in charge of that department call the person back, not you. Hold *them* accountable. I can assure you, they'll get their ass in gear when it starts getting chewed out.

But don't be surprised if they don't want to call. These people are sissies who want everyone else to do their dirty work. They'd never admit to being wrong. Use these people as an example of what NOT to be like. Hold peolple personally accountable for their mistakes. Make them clean up their own messes.

Track Your Call Numbers

Use a call sheet to track your calls. A lot of people think they make tons of calls, but, believe me, they don't.

If you're not on a computerized system that dials for you and keeps track, make a call log. I usually write at the top of my call sheet the industry, calls, contacts, pitch, voice mail, prospect, and sale. I also write at the bottom such things as call backs, contacts, and sales. Keep in mind, a call is when someone picks up the phone and says "ABC Corp."

Dial in 40's

Dial in batches of 40. That's 40 calls an hour. After that, take a small break. Also, don't hang the phone up after each call. Just keep dialing.

No Computer? Use a Tickler File

If you don't have a computer at your desk, use a tickler file for your call backs. Get one that's 1-31 days, and get a monthly one too. When your prospect tells you to call back, just put the call back in the appropriate date and forget about it. Piling up your call backs in a folder or drawer is just plain stupid. I've seen people with hundreds of pieces of paper all over the place, stuck on the walls, in their drawer, on their head, all over the desk. You can't keep track this way. I truly believe that most salespeople lose 10% of their annual income due to poor organizational skills. Make it a point to have an immaculate desk.

Fax Cover Sheet

If your fax cover sheet is 8 x 11, stand it up in your tickler file. About 2-3 inches will be sticking out the top. Write the person's name and company name on the top right corner. A lot of times someone will call before your scheduled call back. Just thumb through your tickler file and in seconds you'll have their info.

Sell 45 Minutes of Each Hour

Want good time management? You should be selling 45 minutes of every hour. That's right, you should be selling 75% of the time, and doing paper work the other 25%. For 45 minutes of each hour you should have the phone in your hand, or

7

headset attached, talking to people. I assure you, by following this time management philosophy, your sales will soar.

Use Headsets

Statistics show people increase productivity by an average of 10% with headsets. Plus, the hands free comfort is great.

Here's how top salespeople think. Monday through Friday is when you work to keep up with your competition. It's on weekends that you get ahead of them. This doesn't mean being a workaholic. I use weekends to read sales literature, look for information on the Internet, etc. I find Sunday nights from 7-9 p.m. a great time to get things done..

Hand-Held Tape Recorder

To save time writing notes throughout the day, you can use a hand held-tape recorder to take notes.

Let Someone Else Do the Cold Calling

Depending on your situation, if you can get an assistant to prospect for you, I suggest you try it. Since I have to read scripts back, play programs back and in general do a lot of paper work, this takes a lot of time off the phone. My assistant comes in Monday-Thursday 10-2. She has a scripted opening statement and a specific script to hand the phone off to me. That's all I want her to do. She makes 30-40 calls an hour. All she does is dial, she doesn't send faxes or do anything else but prospect.

Stand Up Your Files

Don't stack your folders up on top of each other. Get a rack that stands them up. Get the type that's on an angle so you can just glance up and get the folder without having to shuffle through them.

Streamline Your Vocabulary

Don't use 20 words to say something if five will do. Blabbers tend to do this. Example: If the person you're talking to does not qualify for your offer, just tell him he wouldn't be a fit for your product. Thank him for taking your call, and move on. Business owners can't stand talking to salespeople who ramble on endlessly and don't say anything.

3

The Power Of How You Sound

During the first 15-20 seconds you're talking with someone, you're judged as either educated or uneducated. Sound educated.

The way your vocabulary, grammar and diction sounds will have a direct relationship on how much you earn.

Match Their Speed

This next point is so important I can't believe salespeople haven't caught on to this yet. Do you always give your presentation at the same rate of speed? If so, you're losing business every day. You have to talk the same speed as your customer. If they're talking at the speed of light, you talk at the speed of light. If they're talking dead slow, you talk dead slow. Once you start practicing this, I promise, the results will speak for themselves. This takes some practice, so stick with it. It also teaches you phone presence and enhances your listening skills.

Sound Like An Expert

Make sure your customers know you're an EXPERT in your field. Sound confident and speak with authority. You should know your product or service inside out.

Don't End on a High Note

Make sure you don't end your sentences on an up note.

Example: *"Hi, I'm Susan Jones^ ."*

It makes you sound like you're either asking a question or not sure of who you are. A lot of people unknowingly speak this way. Record your calls!

actice Out Loud

Whenever learning a new phrase, word, close, etc., say it out loud. Listen to how you sound and how you say it. Rehearse like an actor. After about a half dozen times, you'll get into a groove of how to say it.

State What You CAN Do

On average, people understand a positively worded statement one third more quickly than a negative statement. To be perceived as a person who knows where he's going and knows how to get things done, always speak positively. If you can't do something for someone, don't say: we can't do that, or that's not our policy. Tell them what you can do. Ever call a bookstore and the book you want isn't in? They always say it's not in, but they can order it for you and you can pick it up in a few days. That's turning a negative into a positive.

Be at Your Best

Various studies have shown that around eighty-six percent of the message your customer gets over the phone is from your tone of voice, inflection, pacing, and volume. You need to train your voice in all of these areas.

Slow Down!

Speak slower when emphasizing important points. Talk half the speed you normally talk. This will get their attention and have them listen better.

Tape Record Yourself

One of the best things you can do to improve your voice, is to record yourself. I also suggest you go to the bookstore and get a book on voice and diction improvement. Get one that also comes with a cassette so you can hear how words are suppose to be pronounced. I'll recommend one in the back of the book.

Baby Your Voice

Keep your voice healthy. Don't shout or put unnecessary strain on your voice. If you're not being heard, adjust your headset. The mouth piece should me right under your lower lip. Drink plenty of water. Do you know that you can lose around a pint of water an hour talking on the phone? Avoid coffee, tea, or colas. They tend to dry out your voice. Carbonated beverages will make you burp. I know that many of you drink coffee when you get to work, but I just wanted to make mention of it.

4

Understanding Personality Types (Yours and Theirs)

In sales you're one of three personality types: Ego, authoritative, or pleaser.

The **ego person** is usually the person who argues the most with other people. They're always being told by people to quit yelling at them. They have zero patience. They give their presentation quick and get to the point. They normally don't like talking in details. They're generally good closers because they're aggressive.

Since ego types vent their frustrations in an outward manner by yelling, they're easy people to read. They want everyone to know of their accomplishments.

If you're one of these types of salespeople, you need to slow down and be more human with your customers and other employees. You normally won't be good at customer service jobs because of your low tolerance. Ego people make very good salespeople once they understand that their aggressive nature could actually be hindering their success, by being rude and too direct with people. You need to control your temper and your sales will take off. Realize that not everyone you talk to knows how your product or service works. Take time with people. Learn to relax a little! Not everybody has an IQ of 500, and wants to work as fast as you do.

Authoritative types are similar to the egos, except they keep everything inside. They really don't care much about winning contests and all the garbage talk in the company. They're very aggressive on the phone, but not very personable. If they called someone back and were told their uncle just passed away, they'd respond back by saying, "That's too bad." They'd then go right into their presentation. Authoritative people need to lighten up a bit. Everything in their career is so serious. They generally read sales books and attend seminars. They know they're good and prove it by their results. Once they add a little more personality to themselves, their sales will take off. It's really ok to laugh once in a while with your customers, really.

The **pleaser** personality types have a hard time accepting rejection. They don't really want to ruffle feathers. They'd rather wait two weeks to hear a no, instead of hearing it today. They want to make everyone happy. This is their downfall. Pleaser personality types are generally at the bottom of the sales group. They do make great customer service reps, and the accounts they do have are built on long term relationships. This is a good person to have in your organization. These people will do better in sales by using a softer, easier approach with people. They need to understand that it's the product getting rejected, not them personally. Teaching them hard, aggressive closing techniques is very uncomfortable for them. They see the ego and authoritative people as being too pushy. If you're one of these types of salespeople, you can increase your sales by learning to be more assertive. Since you easily build trust and rapport with your customers, you're doing them a disservice by not asking them for their business. Get rid of those wishy-washy phrases such as, "*I was wondering if,*" or, "*Did you have a chance to review my information?*"

Tell yourself today that you'll ask for the order more often. In fact, keep a sheet of paper on your desk that reads: how many times did I ask for an order today? Every time you ask, put a check on the sheet. If you spoke to 30 people and only have one check, you know you need to improve your skills. If you're afraid to ask for the order, you're in the wrong profession.

Types of Buyers

Always keep in mind you're selling to 1 of 2 types of buyers. They're either an **overview** or **detailed** buyer. An overview prospect just needs the basics to make a decision. He's probably investigated your product or service and has a good idea about it. Don't bore him with details. On the other hand, if someone starts asking specific detailed questions, talk to him in details. This is important. Always ask yourself if the person you're talking to is an overview or detail personality type. Sell to them accordingly, and you'll make a lot more sales.

Types of Prospects

There are four types of prospects. The first is the person who **sees your product/service as a benefit** to the company. He likes the idea and just simply wants it. These are people we all want to reach. The sale's quick and easy. This is the best prospect.

The second type of prospect is someone who **desperately needs your product/service**. Maybe his old machine can't keep up with production, or is broken down. These people have a genuine need for your offering. Simply solve their headache and you have a sale.

The third type of prospect is someone who **feels everything is ok.** He sees no reason to change things and just wants to keep things the way they are.

The fourth type of person is someone who **would never even consider** your product or service. They don't like it, tried it and hated it, or just simply won't even let you discuss it with them.

The way to be successful is to concentrate on the first two. All prospects fall under one of these four categories. Once you understand that concept, you'll sell a lot more by dealing with the good prospects.

How to Work With Personality Types

There are some personality types you deal with every day. Here's a few ideas to help you sell them.

- **Indecisives.** With the person who simply can't seem to make a decision, be firm and use a little more pressure than you normally would.

- **The chiseler.** He won't buy unless he's getting some special deal that no one else is getting. Toss in a little something, and let him know you don't do these types of things for other people, but you'll make an exception in his case. He'll feel like he's getting more than the rest. He'll buy.

- **Mr. Crude.** He curses, swears, and bluffs. If you're timid, you'll get clobbered. Just relax and go with the flow. He'll run out of steam and buy. He just wants to let you know that you better be on the up-and-up with him. Put up with his vulgar mouth and collect your commission.

- **Mr. or Ms. Moody.** When you spoke to them originally they were all talkative and interested. On your call back you think you're talking to someone else. Just tell them it sounds like they're pretty busy and you'll call back at a better time. Ask them if tomorrow would be better for them. They'll normally say yes in a quick sharp tone. These people need a little more time to develop, but work with them, you'll get them on a good day and they'll apologize for putting you off.

- **The Complainer.** These people whine over everything. Just listen and ship their order. Keep in mind, 10% of the people you won't satisfy no matter what. A good salesperson knows when to get rid of a problem account. Sometimes you just have to fire your customer for the good of yourself and the company.

All prospects want to save time, save money and get rid of their headaches. Help them get what they want.

Reasons People Buy

There are basically two reasons why people buy from a salesperson.

1. They know they have a need for your product/service, and you happened to be in the right place at the right time to get their business.

2. They think of your offer as an opportunity you brought to their attention.

The first group is the easy group to sell to. The second group is a little tougher. They like what you have, but you really have to show them the value of what you can do for them. If you're working on a sale, always make a note to yourself on their folder if the prospect sees your offering as a need or an interest. If they're a need person, give them a good price and close the deal right away. The interest people need proof. Show them how they'll get a return on their investment, how much time they'll save, etc. This person will take a little more time to work, but it's worth it. This is the type of person you want to call every three months for a full year. I've found that about 30-40% of these types of customers will buy during that time.

Emotion vs. Logic

Buying decisions are more emotional than logical. Look around your home and you'll find most of the things you have were bought on emotion, not logic. Appeal to their emotional needs.

Many times people reject your product or service because of personal issues. They don't realize how their decision is affecting other people in the company. Here's a perfect example. Many business owners, particularly small business owners with a handful of employees, don't have a computer. The reason is because the owner thinks it's too hard to learn, or they've been doing just fine without one. That's his personal view.

Meanwhile, his employees may be very knowledgeable about computers. I now make sure the decision maker knows how his decision is affecting other people and the company as a whole. I use the phrase, "Why are you denying ...?"

> **"Tom, why are you denying your employees the opportunity to increase their productivity by 50%?"**

If you sold insurance, you could say,

> **"Irv, why are you denying your family the chance to keep living the life style they're accustomed to if something were to happen to you?"**

For someone trying to get a new product line out,

> **"Frank, why are you denying your customers the opportunity to try this new product out?"**

For a sales force,

> **"Susan, why are you denying your sales reps the opportunity to be competitive and keep up with the rest of your industry?"**

For security systems,

"Bill, why are you denying your family the peace of mind knowing that they can feel safe when you're not home?"

Always let the other person know that their decision will affect other people. Many times this will sway their opinion to look more closely at your offering. Maybe the owner will go to one of the employees and ask them if he did get a computer, would the employee know how to set it up and use it? If the employee said yes, he more than likely would explain the benefits to the owner of having one, since it would make the employees life a lot easier. As human beings, we always look at things from our own personal perspective. That's normal rational thinking. Make sure your prospect understands that his decision is affecting a lot more people than just himself.

Types of Customers to be Aware Of

Here are a couple of types to watch for.

• **The Yes Customer.** This is the person who's agreeing with you through the whole presentation. He's saying yes to this and yes to that. No matter what you say, he's agreeing. Then when you ask for the order, he says NO. If you feel you're talking with one of these people, the best approach is the shock approach. Just stop in the middle of what you're saying and say,

"Jim, why aren't you going to buy this product?"

Or,

"Why aren't you going to use this service?"

This will do one of two things. He'll say he's not interested or he'll start paying attention. Don't play games with this type of person.

• **The Mr. Know-It-All.** You know the type of customer I'm talking about. He thinks he knows more about your product/service than you do. The way to handle this customer is to let him keep blabbing away. Go along with him. Tell him how knowledgeable he is and how he's been doing his homework. Let him talk himself right into a trap. When he's finished, all you have to say is,

"Bob, since you understand all the benefits this will have for you, did you want one or two cases?"

Or,

"We can start the service this Monday." (Start filling out the order form).

Most people won't stop you because it would make them look like a fool. I love the Mr. Know-It-All.

Attach Your Own Personality to the Call

Here's some good insight. Once you attach your personality to a proposition, people start reacting to the personality, and stop reacting to the proposition. The idea is to bond with your customer once he shows an interest in your offer. This nonsense about bonding before they even know what you have to offer is just really stupid. Such as saying things like,

"How 'ya doin today?"

"How's the weather?"

"How about those Yankees?" etc.

Idiot salespeople actually start conversations this way, without even telling the person why they called. They think this is bonding. Give your presentation first. If they're interested in your offer, you can then begin a relationship with them.

5

Tips for Buying Sales Leads

No matter what type of product or service you sell, if you don't have the proper leads, you won't be able to sell it. If you're selling from a list of existing customers, or your marketing department generates leads for you, skip this chapter.

For people who must acquire their own sales leads, it amazes me how much time is wasted on trying to sell to non-qualified buyers. No matter what you sell, you have a target market.

One method of getting sales leads is buying them.

If you're selling to home owners, you can order leads by selecting single, married, married with children, annual income, doctors, lawyers, etc. If you're selling to businesses, you can get: employee size, annual sales, type of industry, franchise or non-franchise, contact name, and even other criteria.

When ordering leads always be sure you get the contact name on them. I can't believe how cheap some business owners are. They'd rather have their salespeople chasing people around to find out who the decision maker is. Wake up out there! Secretaries are taught to screen out anyone who asks who's the owner, or who handles the marketing for the company? I assure you, if you're working for a company that won't even supply you with the contact names, then you're working for a company with a lot of employee turn over and an owner who doesn't respect his sales force.

When calling businesses, always order your leads by saying you want contact names for owner, C.E.O., and president. Forget about the managers' names. Managers can say no, but they can't say yes. If you're working on such a large deal that you have to go through management to get to the top, that's a different story. I'll be recommending books that will deal with

19

that subject. For now, don't pitch managers or secretaries. Also, don't order franchises unless you know for a fact that each store you call can make their own decisions without having to go through corporate.

Also, no branches unless you know the branches can make their own decisions without going through corporate. If you do call on an industry that has franchises or branches, order "headquarters."

My target market is companies with 10 or more employees. No franchises unless the branches can purchase on their own. Headquarters are OK. No manufacturers. Many of them don't get calls from the public and they deal with the same few companies day in and day out. We need companies that get a lot of calls from the public on a daily basis. Insurance companies, body shops, etc.

By knowing exactly what your target market is, you save a lot of time by not making calls to unqualified people. Make sure the leads you order have a contact name!

Tip on Using Your Leads

Check the Weather Channel every morning or get a copy of USA Today, or check one of the weather websites like CNN.com. If you sell nationally, and see that a state is having an earthquake, hurricane, tornado, floods, or just bad weather, don't call those areas.

I can't believe, in 1992, hours before hurricane Andrew hit south Florida, we got a telemarketing call. Any, or almost any literate person would have known not to call then.

Also, be aware of the seasons. Trying to sell swimming pool supplies in Michigan in the middle of winter is going to be a tough sell. As you can see, you can easily put the numbers on your side by using some common sense.

NOTE: I do not recommend those lead disks that have millions of names on them. You have no idea who you're calling. For example, you don't know whether they have 1 or 999 employees, you have no idea of annual sales, decision maker names, and I've found 40% have disconnected numbers. This is a lot of wasted calls. Be sure to ORDER LEADS!

Note: Association Books are ok to use, as long as you're going after your target market. Many of them list sales volume and other important information. It's so important to know your target market. It really makes a huge difference in your sales, and the amount of money you can generate.

6

Dealing With Voice Mail

With modern technology moving forward at a rapid pace, you need to keep up with it on a regular basis. Voice mail can literally be a gold mine for you if you use it the right way. I believe you should only use voice mail as a last resort. If you've made at least three attempts and still can't get through, leave a voice mail. Here are a few tips to consider.

❑ Voice mail may only allow you one minute of time to leave your message. Other systems may have two minutes or more. Start out your call with your name and number.

❑ Always repeat the phone number twice. Once at the beginning, and again at the end.

❑ Speak slow! How many times have you had voice mail messages that you had to keep playing back to get the number?

❑ Say the phone number as if you were writing it.

❑ If calling nationwide, after leaving the number, let the person know if it's Eastern, Central, Mountain or Pacific time.

❑ If you have a toll-free number, leave that. People will call an 800, 888, or 877 number seven times more than a number they have to pay for.

❑ After saying your name and number, tell them what company you are with, and the reason for the call. Write out a script! This is no time for uhms and duhs. I usually say,

"Hello Jim, this is Joe Catal. My number's 1-800-221-4545, calling you at 2:20, that's Eastern time. Jim, I'm with ABC Corporation. We specialize in (NOTE: this is a good time to use your interest creating opening statement which we'll discuss later in the book) **If you'd like to know more about something like this for your company. Please call me personally, and I'd be more than happy to answer any of your questions and send you an information package. That number again is 1-800-221-4545 . I look forward to your call Jim."**

I've found this works equally well when calling homeowners and leaving a message on their answering machine.

❑ Once you write your script, call yourself to hear how the message sounds. Try to say your message in 30-45 seconds.

❑ When filing your voice mail calls, file them by company name, not by the person's name. Often the decision maker will have a manager or secretary call who will have a different name than on your lead. You'll be looking all over for it and probably have to tell the person you don't know who they are. That's not good. If I don't hear back from them within a week, I'll call them. If I get their voice mail again, I'll leave one more message. I've had a good response with leaving a second voice mail if they don't call from the first. I normally tell them I called last week and still haven't heard back, so this will be the last time I'll be contacting them about this opportunity. I make the second voice mail a little on the rough side. Let them know what they're missing out on. I tell them almost 40% of their industry is already using on-hold messages with great results. If they still don't call back, move on.

The KILLER Voice Mail that Gets Me a 50% Return Call Rate

I say,

> "Hello Jim. This is Joe Catal. My direct number's 305-555-1212. I've been trying to reach you for almost two weeks now, but can't seem to catch you in. I think there's a good possibility we may be able to do some business together. In order to find out, I need to speak with you personally. I'll be in my office all day today until 5 p.m. Eastern time. Again, my number's 305-555-1212."

Any business owner who thinks he has a possibility to do business will call you. If possible, don't leave your company name. Also, make sure you know what you're going to say when they call. Be direct and tell them what you do, and why you were calling. I've never had anyone get upset with me for using this technique.

Dump the Call Waiting

Make sure you don't have Call Waiting on your business phone. Use voice mail instead. There's no one more important to you than the person you're talking to. Why put them on hold? It's very rude and unprofessional. With voice mail you can return the call after you've made your sale. If you're guilty of doing this, change it. If you don't change it, call yourself an idiot.

Have Your Own Voice Mail

If possible, you should have your own voice mail so customers can call you direct. I don't like to depend on other people having to give me messages. If someone calls you at nine in the morning, you don't want the receptionist handing it to you at three; you want your messages promptly. If you're a business owner, make sure your people get their messages right away. Speed counts.

What to Say on Your Voice Mail Greeting

On your personal voice mail, ask the person to leave a particular time when they'll be available for your call back. This will help avoid time consuming phone tag. Also ask them to speak slowly when leaving their phone number. You want to make sure you understand it. Remember, 80% of the people out there have never had professional training on how to use a telephone properly.

Don't Pester Them

Don't annoy your prospects by calling them back five times a day. Leave your name or a voice mail. If they don't return your call, wait two days before calling back. Here's a good tip. When leaving your message on voice mail, always say,

> **"If I don't hear back from you by the end of the day, I'll try back before I leave the office."**

This gives you another reason to call.

When They Complain that YOU Don't Have Voice Mail

Here's a good example of turning a negative into a positive. If your company doesn't have voice mail, instead of saying we don't have that, or we're not that modern yet, say,

> **"We do it the old fashioned way, we talk to you personally. How can I help you?"**

Always Leave Your Number

Always leave your number when leaving a voice mail. Often, people will call in while away from the office and check their messages. You should assume they don't have your number with them. Make it easy for people to reach you.

Offer an Incentive for Responding

If you leave a voice mail for someone, you can start out by saying you've called several times but couldn't get through. State the reason for the call, along with your number. You can also leave your web site address. You may want to put a little urgency in your voice mail. Tell them if they respond to your message within 48 hours, and they decide to do business with you, they'll receive a 5 or 10% discount.

Urgency Voice Mail for Existing Customers

This is good to use when you have a special promotion or sale. Make sure you tell them you need to hear from them by a certain day and time, or they'll miss out..

> "Hi Jim, it's Mike Powers over at ABC Office Supplies. I just wanted to let you know we're running a special. Everything in the store is 10% off. If you need any supplies, I need to hear from you no later than Friday for you to get the discount."

7

Getting Past the Gatekeeper

Getting past the secretary does not have to be a long drawn out process of being her best friend. And, you don't need to go to the other extreme, lying and scamming yourself past the screener by telling her that you are with the I.R.S., a friend, it's a personal call, etc.

To get past the screener, you need to sound very authoritative and professional. You want to sound as if you're an attorney calling to collect on a bad debt. Use the firm no nonsense approach. Sounding wishy washy will get you killed.

Screener: "Hello, National Mortgage. How can I help you?"

Sales rep: **"John Smith, please."** (Don't say, "Is John Smith in?" Or, "available") Just say the name.

Screener: "Who's calling?"

Sales rep: **"Joe Catal. John's in, isn't he?"** Or: **"Would you tell him it's Joe Catal, please? Do you know if he's in?"**

Screener: "What company are you with?"

Sales rep: **"Just tell him it's National Systems. He should be familiar with us. I'll hold thank you."** (If he comes to the phone and says he's not familiar with your company, just tell him you do regular mail outs to his area, and continue as you normally would).

In my experience, ninety-five percent of the time that gets me right through. Notice how we didn't blab to her about who we are and what we're calling about?

But what if she asks what the call is about?

Sales rep: **"Would you tell him I'm calling to see if he's interested in expanding the company? I'll hold while you get him. Thank you."**

Or, **"Because of the confidential nature of the call, I'm not at liberty to discuss this matter with anyone other than Jim. Would you tell him I'm on the line please, I'll hold thank you."**

Or, **"I'm calling to see about possibly doing business with him. Can I speak to him?"** (This last one's my favorite, I use it all the time)

If for some reason she keeps on you, just tell her you'll call back. Call back at lunch time when there's usually someone else watching the phones while she's at lunch.

Also try before and after business hours.

I've sold products and services to more than 150 Fortune 500 companies. These techniques work.

If your company name gives away what you do, such as: American Insurance, you might just try saying American Corp., American Services, or use the initials.

If your title is owner, president, vice president, marketing director, etc., use that.

When she asks what company you're with, say, **"Would you tell him it's the President of ABC Corp? I can hold a moment while you transfer me. Thank you."**

A screener will put the President or V.P. through just about every time. If you don't have that title, you could say,

"Would you tell him it's the service manager from ABC Corp? I can hold a moment while you transfer me. Thank you."

NOTE: If you only have five leads to work a week, you may have to get to know the screener to get to the owner. That's an entirely different approach.

8

Effective Openers

If you want to find prospects, you better have a good opening statement. Just calling up to say "Hi," then blabbing away won't cut it. All superstars have worked hours, if not years, perfecting their opening statements.

There are two types of opening statements and two schools of thought on which type is better.

The first type of opening statement is **product** centered. I sell telephone on-hold message systems. I sometimes use this opening.

> **"Hello Jim? This is Joe Catal with R. B. Systems. Jim, we're the people that have been producing the telephone on-hold message programs for the collision industry. I noticed while I was on-hold you had silence on your phone lines. The reason I wanted to speak to you personally, is to see If I can play you a short 30 second sample, to give you an idea of how other people in your industry are using these programs. Do you have a moment to listen?"**

As you can see, this is a straight product call. With this type of opening, I'm only looking for people who are in the market for what I have.

The second type of opening statement is the **benefit** opening. It doesn't mention the product or service, just the benefits. Here's how the exact product above can be sold.

> **"Hello Jim? This is Joe Catal with R. B. Systems. Jim, we specialize in showing body shops how they can enhance their company image, by making sure anytime someone calls in and is placed on hold (like I was), instead of hearing music or silence, they'd be hearing information about your company. The reason I**

> wanted to speak to you personally, was to see if
> I could play you a short 30 second sample to
> see if this could be of any value to you. Do you
> have a moment to listen?"

As you can see, this is giving people a different perspective of your product or service. Both types of statements have their merits. I go back and forth between them. If I'm meeting a lot of resistance on the product opening I'll switch to the benefit opening.

You may have noticed a few things here. Look at how I started: **"Hello Jim?"**

That question mark is there for a reason. I want to get a response from him so I have his full attention. Once he says yes, I pronounce my name and company name *slowly and clearly.* If you constantly have people asking you to repeat your name or company name, it means you're talking too fast or mumbling. I also ask people if they have a moment to talk. Ever since I've included that one statement, my sales have taken off. You don't want to talk to people who don't want to talk to you. Once you say your opening statement, if they're not interested in talking to you, you're not interested in talking to them. It's really that simple. Keep in mind, prospecting is completely different from selling. Focus on 40 calls an hour, and you'll increase your cash flow substantially.

"How Are You?"

Don't use the phrase *"How are you today?"* It makes you sound like a bimbo-headed telemarketer. No one wants to talk to a telemarketer! Just say your opening statement and get to the point. If you want to say something instead of "How ya doin today?," say, *"Thanks for taking my call."*

> "Hello Jim? This is John Smith calling from
> A.B.C Corp. Thanks for taking my call."

Then continue into your presentation.

What if the person tells you they're busy? Often people will say that to get you off the phone. Other times, they may really be interested in what you have, and are busy. How do you know who's for real and who's not? Simply use this statement:

> "I can call you back in 30 minutes, unless you'd
> rather pick another time?"

They'll either tell you to call back in 30 minutes, or tell you to call them tomorrow because they're interested in talking with you, or just tell you to try back another time, click. (That last one is a no interest.)

For those of you who insist on slamming people, and want to keep them on the phone as long as possible until the person hangs up on you, (which I think is totally idiotic), here's a response you can say back before you hear your second "no."

> **"Many of our customers said the same thing at first, until they realized that this was something that could complement the way they do business. Since I have you on the phone, can I just ask you a few quick questions?"**

Or,

> **"Can I at least give you some of our prices? "**

Become a Master Prospector

It's important that you become an expert prospector. Here's a template you can use for an opening statement.

> **"Hello _____? This is** (first and LAST name) **with Co. Name. We specialize in** (benefits). **The reason I wanted to speak with you personally, was to ask you a few quick questions to see if this could be of any value to you. Do you have a moment to talk?"**

Or,

> **"...and if I caught you at a good time, I'd like to ask you a few questions to see if this could be of interest to you. Do you have a moment to talk?"**

An opening statement takes a while to come up with. Make sure you know what your call objective is. Are you trying to close the sale on one call? Do you want permission to send info? Do you want to set up an appointment? Once you know exactly why you're calling, you'll be more focused on what you need to say. Really make it a point to write a good one.

Also keep in mind, not every person you talk to will want to speak with you no matter how good your opening is. Just move on, they're not a prospect.

Don't Hang Up

Whenever you prospect, *never hang up the phone!*

Don't make one call, hang up, take notes and dial again. That's just wasted time. Your goal is to get through your list as quick as possible, and find the buyers. If they're not interested, you don't need to write "not interested" on the lead sheet or card. Your goal is to talk with DECISION MAKERS! not to pitch receptionists. I don't know why it's so hard for people to understand this concept. If you're not making 40 calls an hour, then you're prospecting the wrong way. Forget about the time, focus on the volume. By doing that, the prospects will come.

Never, never, never, start your calls with how are you today! Don't sound like everyone else. Superstars don't start their calls that way. You're calling for their business, make sure they know that. Asking them how they're doing is not bonding with them. That's some idiotic concept that came out of the 60's. Make 40 calls an hour and you'll get the business.

Yes, I know I repeated myself twice. I just wanted to get this point across: No *"How 'ya doin'?"*

9

Listening Aggressively

Before we get any further into the book, it's important that I don't get you too fired up about talking. That's because it's not nearly as important as listening.

People think good salespeople have a gift for gab. That's absolutely false! What they have is a gift for *listening.* Good salespeople don't gab. There are no natural born salespeople. You have to educate yourself and work hard at it.

If a salesperson is talking, that means they are not listening and learning. Many salespeople ramble on thinking they're being friendly. Customers view compulsive talkers as boring time-wasters. Don't be a blabber!

Tom Hopkins says that to be a better listener, the next time you're having a conversation with someone, you should be hearing *their voice* in your head, instead of your own. Try it. When you're talking to someone today, really hear their voice in your head. Good listening builds trust. Without trust you can never make a sale.

The 75% Rule

Always keep in mind, the customer should be talking 75% of the time. The more he's talking, the more he's getting involved. Don't stop a prospect from talking! Listen, listen, listen!

Don't Interrupt

Never interrupt a person while they're talking just because you know what they're going to say. You may know exactly where they're going, but let them speak. It's important to them.

Be Patient

Develop your patience. If you're the type of person who's more concerned about what you have to say than the other person, you need to practice patience. This is also a sign of poor listening skills. Relax and listen. Don't jump right in as soon as you hear a pause.

Let Them Finish

Don't end your customers' sentences for them! This is a horrible habit many people have. Are these people so impatient that they can't even let them finish a sentence? This is pathetic. It shows they have absolutely no listening skills. They're more concerned about what they have to say, than the prospect.

Stay on their Topic

If a customer's talking about a specific feature or benefit, don't change the subject! Don't start moving onto another subject until you've thoroughly answered and satisfied his questions. Many reps go all over the map jumping from topic to topic. Slow down and listen. Talk about what's important to the customer. Just because you think a certain feature or benefit is a major selling point, it may not be to the customer.

NEVER STOP A PROSPECT FROM TALKING!

10

Presentation Ideas

In this chapter I'm sharing lots of ideas on presenting, and other parts of the call.

Ending the Call With Impact

Brian Tracy has a great way of ending a call. Before hanging up you can say,

"In addition to all the guarantees and assurances our company offers, I'll give you my personal guarantee of satisfaction that this will be one of the best decisions you've ever made for your company."

That sounds a lot better than thanks for the order, click. This is the ending I personally use.

Words to Avoid

When talking with business owners don't say the word COST. Say *investment*. "It's just a one time investment of only $400."

Don't use the word CONTRACT. Say *agreement*.

Don't use the word SIGN. Say *ok,* or *approve*.

"I'll fax you the agreement. Just ok it and fax it back so we can get started."

Using Tie-Down Questions

Tie-downs have been around for years. I'll briefly address them. A tie-down is when you end a statement with things like, wouldn't it, wasn't it, isn't it, isn't that right, couldn't it, doesn't it? etc.

Examples:

"Because of the smaller size, it could fit right in that corner, don't you think so?"

"Getting it delivered next Wednesday would be good for you, wouldn't it?"

"That's a pretty color, isn't it?"

As you can see, it's getting people to agree with you. This is a good technique but don't overuse it. There are many tie downs. Sprinkle them through your presentation.

Talk Only About Their Interests

Only talk about the features of your product or service your prospect wants to talk about.If they're only interested in two features, discuss those two features only. Don't bring up the other ten! Many salespeople lose sales by blabbing too much.

Be a Consultant

When selling, be more of a consultant than a salesperson. Be the expert, the go-to person. I can assure you that the fast-talking, one-shot, deal-selling techniques will get you killed. Many times you'll have to talk to several different people. You want all of them to say to one another that you're really knowledgeable and an expert in your field. When it's time to buy, they'll go with you more often than not. Always talk like a consultant, not a salesperson.

They Buy What Your Product/Service Does

Talk about what your product/service *does,* not about what it IS. Really think about that for a minute. Now, explain your product that way to your customer. This is what separates the top producers from the low-end producers.

To Sell at a High Level,
You Need to Be at a High Level Personally

Reality check: Salespeople, particularly newer ones, typically will be most comfortable selling to a person they feel is at the same level as them. If you want to sell to a higher-level customer, you have to develop yourself and work at it. That doesn't mean you have to go to med school to sell to physicians. It means you need to become an expert in your field and sound like it. Are you the type that would feel comfortable talking with doctors, lawyers, executives, etc? Or do you feel more comfortable talking to blue-collar workers? A top producer can sell to both. Bottom line, work to raise your product/service expertise to the level of the people you need to be speaking with, and then convince yourself that you deserve to be selling at their level. People who don't do this are stuck picking up the crumbs at the low levels.

Use Third-Party Examples

Don't be afraid to tell the prospect a story about other people who've had good results with your product/service. People like to hear stories.

Sell What They Feel is the Benefit

A benefit isn't a benefit unless the customer says it is! What may be a benefit to you, may not be to the prospect. You should talk feature, advantage, benefit. Example. When I was purchasing a new car, the salesman started telling me the benefit of driving a stick shift, and how it would give me better gas mileage. That wasn't a benefit to me! I can't stand stick shifts, and I could not care less about the extra two miles per gallon I could get. He should have said that **"the *advantage* of driving a stick shift is ... Do you prefer a stick shift or an automatic?"** This guy never once asked me what I wanted. If you explain a feature, explain the advantage of that feature, and then ask your prospect if that would be a benefit to him. If yes, great, if not, change the subject. From now on think: FEATURE, *ADVANTAGE,* BENEFIT.

And no, I didn't buy the car from him.

Help Them Visualize Ownership

Use the words: *"When you own,"* or *"When you use."*

Example:

> **"When you own this product, you'll never have to worry about it wearing out or breaking like your existing model."**

Or,

"When you use this service, you'll never have to worry about your paper work piling up. Talk to them as if they're already owning and using it."

The Buying Process

Here's a process all business owners and people in general go through when deciding to make a purchase. They ask themselves if they have a need for your product or service, and, do you have the solution to their need. How much will it cost? They are wondering about the risk of buying from you, instead of someone else. If you can fulfill all their needs, you have a sale.

Present With Conviction

Don't talk like you're unsure of yourself. Don't say things like,

"I think it will work for you."

"I'm pretty sure it has that feature on it."

Tell them it will **definitely** work for them. Become such an expert that there's no question someone could ask you about your product that you wouldn't know.

"Do You Work on Commission?"

Sometimes people will ask you if you work on a commission. Tom Hopkins has a great response.

"Yes I do get a commission. My company compensates me for the high level of service I give to my customers. That's what you really want, isn't it? "

Get to the Point Quickly

In phone sales you need to keep your presentation short and to the point. You have about three minutes to say what you have to say. That's why using a script is so powerful. It keeps you from rambling on, and adding words that don't need to be used.

Get the Name of the Buyer

If you don't know the name of the person you're calling, don't say, *"Who's in charge of the marketing for the com-*

pany? Instead, say,

"What's the name of the person who handles the marketing for the company?"

Most of the time they'll just tell you. Then say,

"Is John in?"

If he is, you'll be surprised how often they put you through. If not, you'll know who to ask for the next time you call.

Get Rid of the "Just"

Take the word *"just"* out of your vocabulary. *"I was just calling to see if you received my info." "I was just calling to..."* Be direct! Say:

"I was calling to..."

Number Your Points

Numbering your points is a good attention getter.

"Jim, There are three points I'd like to cover. The first is the efficiency of this service, the second, ..."

Be Honest, But No Need to Say It

Never use the phrase, *"To be honest with you."* Does this imply you haven't been honest? Get rid of this lame phrase TODAY!

Avoid Technical Jargon

Don't talk in technical terms to a prospect unless they talk in technical terms to you. Speak to them so a 12-year-old could comprehend what you're saying. Dazzling someone with all your great technical knowledge is not in your best interest. When I speak to someone about purchasing a Telephone On-Hold system, I don't ask them if they have a KSU box. They wouldn't know what I was talking about. Instead I ask them if they have a phone system that can play music through their phone lines. That, they understand.

Put the Words in Customers' Mouths

Instead of saying we have the lowest prices, say,

> **"Our CUSTOMERS tell us we have the lowest prices."**

It sounds more believable.

Never Bad Mouth Competitors

Don't bad-mouth your competition. It makes you look bad. You can win without doing that. I personally have the attitude that I want to crush my competitor. I want to put them out of business, and steal their accounts. If they're a local company and have a good rep, I'll try to recruit him.

Draw Word Pictures

Use words that create visuals in your customer's mind. Say things like,

> **"It's about the size of a hand-held calculator. It's so lightweight you can put it right in your purse."**

This gives them an idea of size, weight, shape, etc. This is a very important concept. You could literally write an entire book on the subject of visualizations. If someone brought a wrecked car into a body shop, you could say,

> **"We'll have your car looking like you just took it off the showroom floor."**

Now that's a great visual!

More Phrases to Avoid

Never use phrases like,

"Ya know what I mean?"

"Ya follow me?"

"You understand?"

Whether they do or don't, they'll always say yes. Nobody wants to come off as being stupid or dumb. Say,

> **"Does that answer your question, or is there still something you may not be sure of?"**

Or,

> **"Did I explain that clearly enough for you? "**

Get Them to Open Up

If you're talking to one of those people with no personality, who only answers questions yes or no, or you just can't get them to open up, repeat back what they said. If he said our software program is outdated, say,

"Outdated?"

Then shut up. Let him explain himself. If he says the company is expanding, say:

"Expanding?"

This is a good technique to get people to talk and open up. You can also use the phrase,

"Tell me more about that."

Just Ask the Question

Don't ask a prospect if you can ask them a question. You just did! Just ask the question.

Note: Some people do use this technique as a ploy to move the questioning along. They say it generates curiosity, and the person will normally say yes. If you use it, use it sparingly. I occasionally use it.

Get Them to Tell You How They Would Benefit

If you can get the prospect to tell you what a feature or benefit would do for his company—rather than you telling him—that's a lot better. After giving your presentation and understanding your prospect's needs, you can say something like,

"Jack, how much time do you think this feature could save you a week?"

If he says it could save him 10 hours a week, that's a lot more powerful then *you* telling him it could save him 10 hours a week. Mold this to fit your particular needs.

Avoid Tough Questions

Don't ask your prospect questions they can't answer. They'll get flustered and just say they're not interested and hang up. A confused mind always says NO!

They'll Probably Pick the Middle Choice

Studies have shown If you give a person three prices to choose from, they'll generally pick the middle price. Most people can't afford the highest, and they know buying cheap doesn't pay off in the long run, so they'll generally settle on the middle price most of the time.

Help Them Own It

Replace the word "buy" with the word *OWN*.

"When you own this, you'll really love how much time this will save you."

Speak in terms of ownership.

Sell Your Company

When talking with people, don't just talk about your product or service, talk about your company. Let people know you're a reliable company, you've been around for 10 years, mention other companies who use your service, etc. Many people neglect this area.

Transcribe Calls into Great Scripts

You'll know you gave a great presentation when the customer tells you to write up the order! That's why you should record your presentations. You can transcribe them into great scripts. You can purchase telephone recorder links at BusinessByPhone.com for around $20.

Talk Only About What is Important to Them

Don't overwhelm your prospect with irrelevant details. They'll ask you about the details that are important to them. Just answer their questions on those details only.

If It's New, Let them Know

The word "new" is an attention getter.

"I'm calling to tell you about our new deluxe model," "...our new prices," "...our new promotion."

People always want to hear about something new.

Attention-Getting Words

Here are five words that customers will pay attention to.

Increase,

improve,

reduce,

save,

gain.

Sprinkle them through your presentation.

Give Your Recommendation

The word *"recommend"* is a powerful word. People who are unfamiliar with your product or service appreciate it when you can expertly give them advice.

"Jim, I recommend you get twenty cases to start with. I've found that most people in your situation normally use them up in about thirty days. Does that sound good to you?"

You can tweak this to fit any type of product or service you sell.

You'll Love This Idea

The word "love" is a good one to use. For example,

"You'll love how easy this is to operate."

"You'll love how much time it will save you."

Think about that for a moment. If you go on a nice trip somewhere and someone asks you about it, you normally say you really had a great time and loved it.

How to Drop a Name

If your company sells to a big name account that your prospect would recognize, don't say dumb things like, *"We sell tons of these units to ABC Company."* Or, *"ABC Company always buys from us."* Say it this way:

"Are you familiar with ABC Company?"

If the prospect says yes, say,

"We're the people they use for their advertising, office supplies, etc."

That's all you have to say. If the company is one of the most respected in their field, they'll know you must be pretty good to get their business.

Don't Cheapen Your Presentation

Don't use the word *"cheap."* Don't say your products are cheaper. Tell them your product will be a better value to them, or save them a substantial amount of money.

Tell Them About Your Experience

If you've been selling a certain product or service for years, tell your prospects.

> **"I've been with this company for nine years. I have over 500 accounts with many of them being Fortune 500 companies."**

People like to know they're working with a professional.

Don't Complicate Things

If you sell a product that may have to be assembled by the buyer, say things like,

> **"It's so easy to put together, you'll have it set up in five minutes. If you have any questions on putting it together, just call our 800 number and our service department will walk you right through it."**

If it sounds hard for someone to do, they won't buy it.

Be Clear With Your Descriptions

Always speak clearly and concisely, and answer your prospect's questions in detail. Remember, a confused mind always says NO! When a prospect of mine has a telephone system that can play On-Hold Messages through his phone lines, I don't just say he can *use* our message system. That doesn't mean anything to him. Saying that would mean I'm expecting the prospect to believe what I'm saying based on a one-minute call. I explain to them that they have a jack built into their main phone box where a CD player plugs into. They don't need tools to do this, and don't have to call their phone vendor to set it up:

> **"Just plug it in, put the CD in the player, hit**

play and repeat and you're ready to go. If you can plug a lamp in, you can do this."

I then ask the person if they have any questions about the set up. If not, I move to the next part of my presentation. Don't ever assume they know how something works.

A Closing Question

Here's a great line I learned from Brian Tracy to use after your presentation:

"Do you think something like this could be a little more effective than what you're currently using?"

If they say yes, start writing up the order. If they stop you, say,

"Is there something you're still not sure about?"

Always be closing. If you haven't read anything by Brian, I suggest you check out his book *"Psychology of Selling."*

Don't Prove Them Wrong

Never tell a customer he's wrong. If he says something about your product/service that's not true, simply say,

"That's interesting you say that. Where did that information come from? "

Maybe the guy heard it from his uncle, aunt, idiot, etc. Proving people wrong is a sure way to lose a sale. Arguing with them is another.

Get Them to Take Action

Here's a good phrase to use when you want them to take action.

"Is there any reason why ...?"

For example,

"Is there any reason why we can't get started today?"

Tell Them it's a Perfect Fit

When a company fits the perfect market for your product/service, tell them so. With the Telephone On-Hold Message systems I sell, I have a specific market. I ask my prospect if he's getting at least 40 calls a day. I tell them the reason I ask is because you're the type of company we like to target, because you get the volume of calls to make these programs successful. Just 40 calls a day comes out to over ten thousand calls a year. That's a lot of people you can be making extra sales to. So tell them why they're the perfect candidate for your offer.

Assuming is Dangerous

As a salesperson you should *NEVER ASSUME ANYTHING!* When a prospect tells me he can play music through his phone lines, I always ask him what brand phone system he has. Maybe he can do it, but he also may have to spend $1,000 to upgrade his phone system to do it. More sales are canceled because you assumed something rather than investigated it.

Limit Their Choices

Don't give people too many options to choose from. You don't want them telling you they want to review all the different pricing structures, colors, sizes, etc.

Give Them Your Complete Attention

Make sure when you're speaking to someone, you're not doing something else at the same time. Give 100% of your attention to the person. If people sense you're not paying attention to them, you more than likely won't get the sale.

Necessity or Luxury?

Here's a very good question to ask to find out how someone feels about your product/service.

"Susan, do you see this product/service as a necessity or a luxury?"

If luxury, explain to her why it's more of a necessity. A lot of people think my on-hold systems are a luxury. I explain to them the reason why so many people use them is because they generate extra business by getting people to ask them about products and services they may not know they offer.

Use their Name

When you mention a major point in your presentation, say the persons' name.

"Mike, this feature alone will save you $1,000 a month."

By saying their name before a major point, or right before you give the price, you'll have their full attention.

Congratulations!

I don't thank people for buying my product. I *congratulate* them on their decision to expand the marketing of their company. Start congratulating people who buy from you.

Make Them Feel Special

Try and make your customer feel like he's getting something special. I like to use the phrase,

"We normally don't do this, but we'll make an exception for you."

Psychologically they feel they're getting more for their money.

Write Like You Speak

When you write your presentation out, write it as closely as possible to the way you talk. It will keep you sounding natural until you memorize it. Edit it unmercifully so every word counts. And don't forget to put in questions at strategic points to get the person involved.

Tell Them About a Package Deal

The term "package deal" is an attention getter.

"Bob, we have a package deal you might like to know about that can save you some money."

Everyone likes package deals. We all know they save us money, so we'll be more apt to listen. The word "deal" by itself is not a good word to use. That's the word scam artists use. *"I got a deal for ya."* Take the word deal out of your vocabulary, and replace it with *package deal.*

Great Words to Use

The word *"magic"* is a good word to use, especially when put together with the word *"new"*.

"This new cleaning solution works like magic."

The word *"easy"* is another great word.

"It's so easy to use."

"It's so easy to put together."

Here are some words that psychologists say have persuasive power.

you,

money,

save,

new,

easy,

results,

proven,

guarantee,

free,

love,

help.

Sprinkle them through your presentation.

Speak With Conviction

Don't use words like *"I think,"* or *"maybe."* They make you sound unsure of yourself. People don't buy from people who aren't confident. Know your product/service inside out!

When They Already Have a Vendor ...

You may want to try this the next time someone tells you they have a vendor.

"John, I realize you have a vendor, but if I could show you that our prices could possibly save you up to 20%, would you be interested?"

Anytime they say they already have anything, remember the phrase, **"But If I could show you how to... would you be interested?"**

Don't Sell a Product

Good salespeople don't talk about products, they talk about *concepts*. Get them thinking and dreaming.

Build Urgency to Act Now

You should have urgency built into your presentation.

- If they order today, they can get a 10% discount.

- If they don't order today, prices will be going up.

- The sale ends today, etc.

How can you add urgency to your presentation so buyers are motivated to buy now?

They'll Talk if They are Interested, But Keep it Tight

If someone's interested in your offer, keep in mind the average person will stay on the phone with you for about 15 minutes before they want to get off. Keep your presentation tight, and remember the time factor. It will help keep you from rambling.

The Three Stages of Mastering Your Presentation

There are three stages to learning your presentation. The first is the learning phase. This is where your first week or two you stumble and stammer.

The second is where you know it, but still need to read it because you don't have it memorized. Most people get stuck on the second phase.

In the third phase you have it memorized so well you can say it in your sleep. It's so ingrained in you that it becomes second nature. It's so important to get to this phase, because it lets you concentrate on other points of the call such as closing signs and better listening. If you've been reading your script longer than 30 days, you're stuck in phase two. Here's how to handle this problem. Take your presentation and put it in your drawer. It's going to be scary at first, but you'll realize you can do it. Just keep a sheet of paper in front of you with headings of important points. Glance at it just to make sure you didn't leave anything out. This also goes for your opening statement. Memorize it and start sounding like you're calling to have a conversation, not give a presentation. You'll never achieve a high level of sales if you can't give a presentation without reading it.

Promote the Benefits of YOU

Don't forget to sell yourself to the prospect. I let them know I've been in the industry for years, have a book out, have worked with many people in their same industry, and some of the large Fortune 500 accounts I have. They know they're working with a professional.

A good presentation has a mix about your product, company, and yourself. Make sure you're not leaving any of those out.

Avoid Repeating the Same Words

Make sure you don't have the bad habit of saying certain words and phrases repeatedly. Things like,

basically,

the reality is,

oh really,

that's great,

let me tell you, etc.

A couple of times is fine, three or more times and you have a bad habit. What words or phrases do you need to cut down on?

Expand on Their Problem

If someone tells you that your product/service could help solve a problem, expand on that. Ask them what type of problems they're having. Who else might it be affecting. Is it causing them to lose money or time? Make them realize the seriousness of their problem. People make changes when they have pain. Always remember that.

"Oh?"

A great word to use is: **"Oh?"** If you call someone back and they decided not to buy, just say, **"Oh?"** Then shut up! They'll start explaining themselves. For example, if they say, "My partner shot it down."

"Oh?"

Ask Them to Tell You More

A great phrase to use is *"Tell me more about that."* This could be used in a number of instances.

"We're thinking of expanding."

"Tell me more about that."

"We're having trouble getting our supplies delivered on time."

"Tell me more about that."

Answer, Then Ask Again to Keep Control

The person asking the last question is in control. Don't just say yes to a question or answer a question and then shut up. That's putting the ball back into their court. Answer it and ask another question back. It's your responsibility to keep the conversation moving. Write out the types of questions you need to ask people. This is a key point you need to understand. If you answer one of their questions with a yes, and then shut up, the next thing they'll say is to send them info. This is part of the selling process very few people understand. Whenever someone asks you a question, answer it, and ask another question back. With practice this will become easy. This is a key secret of all top producers.

Tell Them Exactly How They Will Benefit

Here's a good phrase: **"Which means to you ..."**

"Jim, we put our On-Hold Program on a compact disc, which means to you that you'll never have to worry about it wearing out or breaking like tapes do."

"We ship everything overnight, which means to you that you'll always have this in stock."

Kids Should "Share." You Don't Need To

Don't use the word "share."It's been beat to death. I just want to share a concept with you to see if you'd be interested. I'd just like to share...

Just tell the person what you want to do and **do** it.

Don't Rush

Don't give a rushed presentation. Sometimes a person will tell you they're interested in what you have, but they're busy. Don't try to tell them it will only take a minute and launch into a 100 mile-per-hour presentation. Schedule a better time to call back. Rushing through a presentation is guaranteed to get you a no.

Always Give the Full Treatment

If you have a friend or relative who wants to purchase your product/service, always give them a full presentation. Don't water it down because you know them.

The Joke is On You

Don't tell stupid jokes to prospects. Many old timers think this is a way of bonding. The only joke is on you ... being told they're not going to do business with you.

Bring Up the Objection First

If you keep getting the same objection or two over and over, just put it in your presentation to avoid it. To avoid the "shop around" objection I typically hear, I tell the person,

> **"If during the next week while we're produc-ing your program, you think you can find a bet-ter offer/price than ours, fax me their proposal and we'll match it."**

What objections do you normally get that you can put into your presentation?

Become the Expert in Your Business

If you work a specific industry, read articles on it. Let prospects and customers know that you keep up with their industry. Tell them stories of how other companies or people like themselves solved problems or increased sales. Lead them to web sites they might like, or tell them about a publication they might like to look at. Always think of ways to give your customers added value. Let them know they're getting more than just a product or service, let them know they're getting you!

Calling yourself an "expert" in your field is good to say to prospects. Another good word to use is "specialist." It gives the psychological effect that you specifically work with that type of company or person only. Doctors use the term specialist. People automatically associate that term with authority.

Know Why You Are Asking

Don't just ask questions to ask questions. Ask questions that will give you important information that will move the sale forward.

Ask About the Past, Present, and Future

When speaking to a customer, ask questions that deal with the *Past, Present, & Future.* Here are some examples:

> **"How did you choose your last vendor?"** (Past)

> **"How are you keeping up with all the paper work?"** (Now)

> **"Do you see your company expanding during the next year?"** (Future)

How can you talk to your customers with past, present, and future questions?

Ask Them About Inaction

If someone really needs your product or service, a great question to ask them is,

> **"What's going to happen if you don't make a change?"**

Sometimes doing nothing may be more costly than your product.

Point Out the Quality

Having a high quality product or service is important to your prospect. If you're selling a service, the benefits you want to talk about are the expertise and knowledge of the people performing the service being sold. If you're selling a product, you want to talk about benefits relating to quality, durability, tested results, etc.

Needs and Wants

There's a difference between "needs" and "wants". Decision makers buy what they need, from someone who understands what they want. Ask good questions and make sure they understand you know what they want.

They're Buying YOU

Most decision makers are more interested in the person they're buying from than in the product or service they're buying. The reason is that decision makers are always looking to build long-term relationships with people who can help their business grow. Ask yourself, would you want to do business with someone on a regular basis whom you don't like? Understand their long-term vision and goals, and you'll make more sales.

True, to be successful you have to be persistent. Nevertheless, top producers know credibility is much more powerful . People buy from someone who's more credible.

Tell Them You Don't Have Competition

If someone asks you about your competition, tell them you don't have any! That shows confidence and conviction in your product and your company. Then just continue with your presentation.

Avoid Red

Never use the color red on your proposals. Red means stop, loss, caution, look out, etc. If you want to use color, use blue, green, yellow high liter, etc. IF YOU USE RED, YOU'RE DEAD!

Don't Be "Sorry"

Take the word "sorry" out of your vocabulary. Use the word "apologize" instead.

Ask About the "Potential"

A good question to ask a customer after your presentation is,

>"Can you see the potential of this product/service?"

>"Can you see the potential of this investment?

>"Can you see the potential time this could save you? "

Get Them Involved

Get your customer involved with your presentation by having them write things down. The more involved they are, the better chance of you making a sale.

Get Them Feeling Instead of Thinking

Don't use the phrase: what do you think? People buy on emotion, not logic. A better phrase is,

>"How do you feel?"

>"How do you feel about something like this?"

Would You Buy From Yourself?

Would you buy from you? This is a good mindset to have when giving your presentation. You'll talk more about the benefits. If you can't sell yourself on your offer, how can you sell someone else? Hmmm?

Ask Them If They Have Experience With Your Product or Service

Ask people if they ever used your product or service in the past? If they have, ask them why they stopped using it. What did they like about it? What would have had them keep using it? A lot of people I talk to have used On-Hold Messages. When I ask these questions, I realize most were using cassettes that wore out and broke. When I explain the technology has changed and the program is now on a compact disc, many will listen.

Speak Their Language

Try to throw in a few words they use. If they say they want to fly out of work early. You can put that in your presentation by saying something like,

"... and with the time you'll save, you'll be able to fly out of the office early on Fridays."

People who talk similarly to you seem to feel like they're closer to you.

Have a Fascination

The word *fascinating* is an unusual word that you may be able to fit into your presentation.

"What you'll find fascinating about our/the..."

This statement can be used for any type of product or service. Use it when describing benefits.

Be Glad To

Substitute the words "I'll have to," with

"I'd be more than happy to..." or,

"I'd be glad to..."

When you say I'll have to, it sounds like you're saying it's something that you have to go out of your way to do. It sounds like you're doing something you don't want to. It's a negative statement. With the On-Hold Messages I sell, often I have to call the prospects phone vendor. I say,

"Jim, if you give me your vendor's phone number, I'd be more than happy to give him a call for you, and get back to you later today on this."

That sounds much better than saying *"I'll have to call your vendor."*

Give Your Recommendation

The word "recommend" is powerful. After you've given your presentation and answered their questions, tell them what you recommend, it puts you in an authoritative position. Doctors, lawyers, mechanics, etc. recommend. We generally take an expert's recommendation. It's also powerful because you're now speaking like a consultant, not a salesperson. I say,

"Based on what you've told me, I recommend that you use a low key conversational program. The reason being is that you're a smaller company and can give better personalized service than those bigger companies. Do you feel the same way?"

As you can see, I also asked a closing question, but in a non confrontational manor. If the person agrees with me, I start writing the order. What have you been recommending to your customers?

Read To Them

If you have testimonial letters (which you should have), read them to the person while they're on the phone with you.

"Frank, let me read to you what Jim Jones over at Pickle Vendors said about us ..."

Then start reading the letter. Make sure it's short and to the point.

Ask About What They Desire to Achieve

Here's a good question to ask someone.

"What are you trying to achieve?"

If they tell you they need a larger copier or better software, ask them (before telling them how great your company is and you have every product on the market) what they're trying to achieve. It's a good question to get them talking. Besides, how would you know what to recommend without first finding out what they want?

Quantify the Problem

"How often does that happen? "

This is a good question to ask when people mention a problem.

"Our deliveries have been coming late."

"How often does that happen?"

"Our computers keep crashing."

"How often does that happen?"

This gets them to start realizing how serious the problem is. A definite plus for salespeople.

Ask Why That is Important

This phrase should be in every salesperson's arsenal:

"Why is that important to you? "

When someone says to me, "What If I want to change my messages more often?" I ask them why that's important to them. Most reps would blab about all the different programs they have available. Remember, you can't answer a question or an objection until you understand why they're asking it!

"I need delivery twice a month."

"Why is that important to you?"

"We need to be moved in by the first of May."

"Why is that important to you?"

This will uncover problems that you can enhance on. As salespeople, we're always looking to increase a persons pain before we offer the solution.

Find Out the Real Reasons

Here are a few questions to ask someone who's still hesitating.

"What concerns do you still have?"

"What's causing you to hesitate?"

"What are you still unsure of?"

These types of questions will get most people to open up and bring out the real objection.

Get Specific With the Benefits

Instead of telling people you have great service or fast service, be specific and explain it to them.

"The reason our service is so fast is because we ship everything overnight."

"The reason our customers tell us we have great customer service is because we can have a repairman at your site within the hour."

Don't just tell people they'll save money or time, explain how.

Get The "But" Out

Substitute the word "and" for "but."

"We can ship it today, but it won't get there until Friday."

That sounds negative.

"We can ship it today and have it to you by Friday. That would work for you, wouldn't it?"

That sounds a lot better, plus you're adding a tag on for agreement.

Review it On Tape

When writing a proposal, read it back into a tape recorder and you'll find any awkward spots.

Who Else Can Benefit?

Ask yourself if your product or service will affect other people or departments in a positive way. When I sell a Telephone On-Hold program to someone, I tell them that every division will be selling for you. If they call the bookkeeper and she puts them on-hold, people will hear info about your company. Think how your product or service can benefit other people of the company, save time, money, etc.

11

Exercises to Help Plan Your Calls

Here are a collection of exercises you can do to help plan for your calls.

Why Do People Buy From You?
List all the reasons why someone should buy your product or service. Add those reasons to your presentation. If you're a manager or an owner, you can make a game out of this with all the employees. On Friday before you leave, or Monday morning, go over the reasons with the group. It gives people ideas and concepts they may not have thought of.

What Results do You Provide?
When talking to a prospect about your product/service, instead of talking in benefits, talk in terms of *results.* Really think about that! What results does a person get from your product/service? Put those results into your presentation. If you're a manager or business owner, you can get the whole company to participate in this exercise.

What Problems Do You Solve?
Ask yourself, **"What problems do my product/service solve?"** Write them out and put them in your presentation. This is another exercise that can be done by everyone in the company. Review the answers with the group.

List Out Your Objections
If you never want to be stumped on an objection again, sit down and write out all the objections you get. There are usually about six. Then take your favorite responses from this

book and use them. Keep in mind, one response might be able to be used on more than one type of objection.

Address Their Fears

All buyers have three basic fears.

1.Buyers are afraid they'll lose money or not get their money's worth.

2. Buyers are afraid the product or service isn't as represented or not worth the price.

3. Buyers are afraid of what others might think. Maybe they think other people will ridicule or mock them.

Look at each fear a buyer has, and write out what you can put into your presentation, or how you can assure him he doesn't have to worry about these concerns.

Can They Use Your Product or Service in Different Ways?

Does what you sell only work one way? Can you adjust it? Use it a different way? Can you present it in a different light? A different type of industry or person? Since I sell an audio product, the potential is endless. Audio brochures, audio catalogs, etc. Are there any other ways people can use your products or services? Look through the Sunday paper, and look at ads that are selling products and services in a different light. Think of all the ways you can use a paper clip!

What Differentiates You?

Write out all the reasons you can think of that differentiates your product/service from someone else. If you and a competitor have the same product at the same price, you need to differentiate yourself. Saying you have great customer service doesn't count—everyone says that. Here are some ideas I use.

• I tell them that we specialize in producing programs for their industry.

• Our script writers have over twenty five years combined experience writing scripts for their industry.

• I let them know of Fortune 500 companies we've done business with.

- I tell them I've written a book. (This almost always guarantees me a sale, the credibility is great.)

I'll use any weapon I can to crush my competition. This is a good exercise to practice with a group. This one exercise alone could literally make you thousands of dollars. The minute you can tell a prospect four or five reasons why you are different than your competitors, you're light years ahead of them.

A great book I recommend on differentiating your product or service is *"Differentiate or Die,"* by Jack Trout. ISBN 0-471-35764-2.

12

Dealing With Mid-Level Managers

One of the most important keys to success in sales is en-suring you are talking to someone who can buy from you. Lots of reps waste tons of time speaking with people who can't make the ultimate decision. Here are some tips to help in this area.

Sell Safety and Fear

When working with managers, sell them on safety or fear. Let them know you've worked with other people in their same situation, and you'll make them look good. You understand how important his project is, and if it turns out bad he's the one on the hook. Give him comfort in knowing that he's in good hands. On the other hand, if he's dragging his feet and nothing's happening, throw a little fear into him. Say,

>**"Jim, we've been trying to get this done for over a month now, and I get the feeling you really don't want to do this. I'll tell Bob (the owner) that you feel this wouldn't be good for the com-pany, and that we've decided not to do busi-ness."**

He'll have a heart attack! He's thinking unemployment. I assure you, you'll become a top priority. Always be thinking fear and safety when working with middle management. This single concept alone is worth thousands of dollars.

Be Sure They Are Sold First

If someone has to run your offer by someone else, and there's no way you can get access to that person, say,

>**"If it were your decision, would you go ahead with this?**

If they say yes, say,

"What do you personally like about it?"

Then ask them if they would tell that same thing to the person they're going to. Any time someone else has to give your presentation for you, the odds are really stacked against you.

When It Seems They are Too Busy ...

If you're working with a manager who never seems to be able to get hold of the decision maker to review your proposal, say,

"Susan, would it help if I spoke to Bob directly?"

Or, **"Would it save you some time and work if I spoke to Bob directly?"**

Reality check: If they say no to this, you need to pin them down on when they'll be speaking with him. If they can't tell you, they may not be sold on your product or service.

Compliment the Manager

Many times an owner or CEO will want what you have, and tell you to work out the details with his manager. When he does sign off on it for you, tell the owner you liked working on the project with his manager. If you happen to be on a speaker phone and the manager hears you say that in front of the big man, you just made him feel like a million bucks. That's good for a long term relationship.

Be Sure You're Talking With a Buyer

Make 100% sure you're working with the REAL decision maker. Often managers act like they're the boss, but have no authority to buy at all. Here's a good question to ask.

"Bob, are you alone the only decision maker on this, or would there be anybody else that would have to agree with this?

If they've been impersonating the real decision maker, this gets them off the hook. In my presentation I say,

"John, the only two requirements we ask of you to get started is, 1. You're the person who can actually make this kind of decision for the com-

pany without getting final approval from anyone else, and, 2. You can afford it at this time. Do you meet those requirements?"

It's direct and to the point, but it works. It doesn't make sense to go through the entire sales process, and the day you go to ship your product you find out you're not even dealing with the decision maker.

13

Closing Strategies and Techniques

You can master every other aspect of sales, but unless you can close you'll be missing out on dollars. Here are some closing tips for you.

Record Your Calls

No matter how much you read and study, the only true way to become a top producer is by recording your phone calls. Some people are amazed when they discover how they ramble on and miss closing opportunities. If there's only one thing you learn from this book, learn to record your calls. You can listen to them on the way home from work. Some people even transcribe them. What a great way to develop a script. (You can get the Recorder Link to tape your phone calls at *www.BusinessByPhone.com/reclink.htm*)

Close on Low Risk

Use low risk as a selling point. For example,

• You've been in business 10 years.

• Name large companies that use your service.

• You'll be there if a problem arises.

• No money up front.

• 30 day invoicing, etc.

Don't you feel more comfortable making a purchase from a store that would give you a full refund or help you with a problem? People will generally pay a little more for that type of security. From now on, you're the *least risk vendor.* This is a key technique. Every top producer uses it.

You're a Problem Solver

Always be thinking in terms of "solutions" Top producers are great problem solvers. Put a 3 x 5 card on your desk that reads: SOLUTIONS.

Get Them Off the Fence

Here's a good question to ask someone who's sitting on the fence.

> **"What would you absolutely have to be convinced of in order for you to go ahead with this?"**

This question will get them to tell you the real objection. If they can't answer you, they're not a prospect. As we all know, the longer a deal sits around, the chances of it going through go down dramatically.

Get Their Opinion

Here are three little words you need to memorize.

IN YOUR OPINION.

> **"John, in your opinion, do you see this as being a benefit to your company?"**

> **"In your opinion, do you feel this would be better than what you're currently using?"**

This works best after you've given your presentation. Most people won't refute their own opinions. Do you?

Trial Closing Ideas

Here are a few trial closes.

> **"How does this sound to you?"**

> **"Does this make sense to you?"**

> **"Is this what you had in mind?"**

> **"Can you see this as an improvement over what you're currently using?**

These questions will give you an idea of how interested the prospect is.

Asking for Credit Card Payment

If you need to get a credit card number after you've written up the order, say,

> **"Jim, I have all the information I need to process your order. Are there any other questions I can answer for you before I let you go?**

If the prospect says no, then say,

> **"Good. Now to get started, all I need is a credit card. I'll hold while you get it.**

> Or, **"Now to get started, all I need is a major credit card. Which one did you want to put that on? "**

Then just shut up! If a business owner tells you she doesn't have a credit card, without missing a beat, say,

> **"That's ok. I'll have Fed-X swing by and pick up a check."**

If she says no to both of these options, she's either not the decision maker, or you slammed her and she has no clue what she's buying.

Reassure Them

Sometimes a customer wants to do business with you, but he's a little leery about doing business over the phone and out of state. Say,

> **"If after 30 days you're not completely satisfied, call me personally, and I'll give you a full refund, no questions asked, ok?"**

They're just looking for a little reassurance. This is the same technique the infomercials use. I've never had anyone call back and ask for a refund.

Be Simple and Direct

Here's a direct close. After giving your presentation, if a customer tells you they like what you have to offer, just say,

> *"Since you like it so much, why don't you get it? "*

It's so direct and simple, often the customer will just say ok!

Small Decisions Can Get Big Sales

Ask for small decisions. This is very important to understand. Instead of asking someone to make a large decision, a secondary question will usually do the trick. I read where a real estate salesman sells million dollar homes by selling people the mail box. If the prospects are interested and he knows they want the house, he'll say,

> **"How would you like your name on the mail box to appear, 'Mr. & Mrs. Jones,' or 'Bob & Mary Jones?'"**

When they tell him which they prefer, they just made a million dollar decision.

When I sell my On-Hold Message systems and I know the person wants what I have, I say,

> **"I noticed the name of your company is ABC Collision. Is that the way you'd like them to say it on the program, or do you answer the phones a different way?"**

When they tell me, that means they've bought. I use this technique on every single sale I write. This is one of the best closing techniques I've ever encountered.

Why Not?

Here's a neat little close. After you've filled out the order form, you can say,

> **"I have all the information I need from you. Is there any reason why we can't get started today?**
>
> Or, **"Any reason why we can't ship it today?"**

Most people will follow your lead and tell you to go ahead with it.

Get Specifics

Always clarify what they mean if you're not sure. If they say they can't buy now because they're going through changes, ask specifically what changes. If they won't speak to you about specifics, you probably don't have a serious buyer.

Don't Wait for More Questions—Close!

After giving your presentation and your customer doesn't have any more questions, say,

"John, you sound to me like you understand everything there is to know about this, and since this is completely risk free to you, why don't you give us a shot?

Or: *"Why don't you give it a try, ok?"*

This is a friendly close.

Give the Desired Choice Second

Whenever you give a person two choices, always give them the choice you want them to pick second. Example:

"Would tomorrow at three be good, or would one be better? "

Most people will choose one.

"We can C.O.D. it. Or would a credit card be better for you?"

The Alternate Choice Close

The majority of top phone reps use the "Alterative choice close." Although it's been around for a while, I highly recommend you use it. It's successful because it works on human nature.

Example:

"Do you want delivery on Monday or Tuesday? Will that be cash or credit card?"

The minute you start hearing buying decisions, you can start to use it.

Ask if they Have Questions

After your presentation say,

"Jim, that's really all there is to it. Do you have any questions? "

If they have a question answer it and say,

"Do you have any other questions?"

If they don't, just start filling out your order form. If they stop you, just say,

"Is there still something you're not sure about?"

You'll be surprised at how many people will just say no, and keep giving you the info. When you start taking info down, this is a great time to use the alternative close technique.

"Would you want one or two cases?"

"Do you want it shipped to your office or warehouse?"

They Expect You to Ask

Very few people will volunteer an order. They expect the salesperson to ask for it. Don't let them down. You're only doing them a disservice if you do.

Close on Their Buying Signals

If you sell a product that has to be delivered, (such as furniture) and the prospect asks you if you deliver, don't just say yeah. Ask them when they'd like it delivered. When they give you a date, they just bought. I would also come back and ask if the morning or afternoon delivery would be best for them.

If you've been in sales any length of time, you've probably heard of the "take-away close." If you know a person's really interested in what you have, you can say,

"This is really one of our best sellers. I don't know if we have it in stock. Can you hold a moment while I check?"

The person's ready to buy now! She's anxious.

Better yet, if your stock is low, come back on the line and say,

"Mary, you're in luck! We have just one (or whatever number) **left, and can get it to you by Wednesday. Would morning or afternoon delivery be good for you? What credit card did you want to put that on?"**

Salespeople use this on us all the time and it always works. We always want the last one, always! It seems to have more value to us.

Ask if They Have Ever Considered Your Product or Service

Ask your prospect if they've ever considered using your product or service, or your type of product/service. If they say yes, immediately respond back with,

> **"What's been keeping you from going ahead with it?**

Many will just say they've been busy and never gotten around to it. I personally ask this question to every single person I talk to. From that point on, I tell them exactly how we work and ask them for the order.

If the prospect says he's never considered using your type of product or service, explain how other companies/people similar to him have been using it to save money, make money, save time, etc. Memorize these two questions. They're extremely powerful, and the results are astonishing.

Ask if It Makes Sense

I like to use the phrase,

> **"Does that make sense to you? "**

> For example, **"Joe, since this is an audio product, in order for you to make a decision on it, you'll need to hear it before we ship it. That makes sense to you, doesn't it? "**

It's a nice tie-down, isn't it?

Listen for the Problems

Always be aware of the word "problem." If a customer uses that word, get him to discuss it fully. You want him to recognize his pain. If he says he has a problem with productivity, ask him what type of problem? How's it affecting other departments or people? The more he realizes he needs to do something, the more he'll listen.

Some Trial Closes

Here are a few non-offensive trial closes.

> **"How would that work for you?"**

> **"Does that sound good to you?"**

> **"Bob, we can wrap this up today. Does that**

"sound good to you?"

"Would that work for you?"

Get Comfortable With Silence

Whenever you ask your prospect a question, shut up and let him answer it! I hear reps shooting out 2-3 questions at a time, never giving the person a chance to answer the first one.

FACT: Most salespeople are scared to death of silence on the phone. My personal best is going one minute 27 seconds without saying a word after asking for the order. The person at the other end said, "After thinking about this, it really does make sense."

The reason there's silence from the prospect's side is because they're serious about purchasing your product. They just need a moment to think of any questions they may have. So shut up after asking a question, particularly a closing question.

Objections Do Not Always Mean Resistance

Just because someone is giving you an objection doesn't always mean they're not interested. They may very well be ready to order. They just need your assurance that they're making the right decision.

Get Them to Move Forward

If you're talking with someone who you feel really wants your product/service and he's just afraid to go ahead with it, say,

"I know how you feel, you're not sure if this will work for you. Isn't that true?"

Or, "I know just how you feel. You're not sure you'll get a return back on your investment. Isn't that true?"

Most will say yes. Then say,

"In that case, why don't you get it and test it out yourself. Let the results make your decision. That's the way to handle this, don't you agree?"

You could add that your product comes with a 30-day money back guarantee, and if they're not satisfied they can call you back personally for a full refund.

You Can Close Any Time

Always be aware that there's not one particular time to close in your presentation. You don't have to wait until after your presentation to ask for the order. If you hear buying signals half way through, start writing up the order. Always be listening for closing signals.

Another Soft, But Effective, Trial Close

After giving your presentation, a good trial close is,

"Can we be any fairer than that to try and earn your business? "

It's a soft sell close, but it's very powerful.

Ask After You Answer

As a general rule, you should always ask for the order after you answer an objection. Most low-producing sales-people only ask for the order once—pros ask an average of three times. That doesn't mean asking for the order three times as soon as you say your opening statement and the prospect says no. Remember, if they're not interested in talking to you, you're not interested in talking to them. Thank you and good-bye.

Help Avoid Buyer's Remorse

If you sell a high-ticket item, I'm sure you've had people call back the next day and cancel. We all know that lousy feeling, and it happens to all of us. Here's a good story to tell people that will really keep that buyer's remorse to a minimum. Really grasp the concept of the story and then apply it to your situation.

"Melvin, I want to let you know you're making a good decision. If you're like most people, you'll probably go to bed tonight and start wondering if you did the right thing. It's kind of like the feeling you get when you buy a new car. No matter how much research you did, (even if

you got the best deal in town), you'll still stay up all night thinking about taking it back the next day. But after you start driving it around and your friends and family tell you what a nice car you have, and what a good price you got, you'll start realizing you really did do the right thing, and you'll start feeling good about yourself. This is the same thing. Once you start using this new machine for a couple of weeks, you'll realize just what a good decision you made. So, go home tonight and feel good about yourself for finally making the decision you know you should have made long ago, ok?"

Fair Enough?

A good statement is,

"That's fair to you, isn't it?"

This works good when you're ironing out those details and they're asking for some small concessions.

There's No Room for the Timid

There's no place in selling for people who are too timid to ask for the order. Just as a lawyer or a doctor has a responsibility to steer his client in the right direction, it's your job to steer your customer into making a right decision. Would anybody in their right mind listen to a sales presentation if they weren't interested? So, what's stopping you from asking?

Ask if They're Sold

Here's a good phrase I got from Zig Ziglar. After your presentation say,

"Joe, have you got yourself convinced yet, or is there still something you're not sure about?"

More Closing Lines

Here are a few good closing statements.

"So why don't you go ahead and give it a try?"

"Lets go ahead with this, ok?"

"Why not give us a shot and see what we can

do for you, ok?"

Create Urgency

Here's a good urgency question. If people order from you on a regular basis, and tell you they'll order a certain product the next time they call, say,

> **"You can do that, but I can't guarantee it will be in stock at that time."**

> Or, **"You can do that, but I can't guarantee it will still be on sale."**

Most will just tell you to add it to the order.

Tell Them How Many Other Smart People are Out There

It's a good idea to let people know how many others have bought from you. For example, I say,

> **"Lou, almost 35% of your industry's already using these programs with great success. I find it hard to believe there's that many idiots in your industry, don't you?"**

You'll get a laugh out of this from the customer. You're making your point in a fun and unusual way. I promise, they won't get upset with you for saying that. Say it in a light tone of voice. Or you can say,

> **"Don't you find it hard to believe that all those people made the wrong decision?"**

Sounds Good?

Here's a good phrase to use for just about anything.

"Sound good?" For example,

> **"Tom, we can have the delivery to you tomorrow. Sound good?"**

> **"We can wrap this up today, does that sound good to you?"**

This is a very friendly persuasion technique.

Ask if it Works for Them

Another good question is, *"Would that work for you?"*

"If I could have this to you by Wednesday, would that work for you?"

Everyone Wants to be the Survivor

When you run into one of those people who absolutely NEEDS what your offering, don't try to sell them on products and features. Sell them on survival!

"What will happen if you don't get your orders out on time?"

"Have you been losing accounts because of the problem?"

"How long have you had this problem?"

The only thing this person is interested in, is getting through his ordeal. If you were a caterer and someone called and said they have an emergency, and need catering for 100 people in two days, you'd sell them on how you could help them. Make suggestions on foods, desserts, etc. Let them know that even on such short notice you'll have everything running smoothly for them, and that they can count on you. Also, for emergency service you can charge more. We all pay extra for quick, immediate, or emergency service. We do it because we're desperate and don't care about the extra few dollars. We just want to get through our bad situation.

Be Aware of Age Differences

Always be aware of the age factor with your customers. Since you're on the phone and can't see them, you have to be guided by how they sound. People from different eras buy differently. These days, everything is speed, fast, right to the point. This is normally not the way a 60-70 year old will buy. In their time, it was about taking time to develop relationships. If you're talking to someone who's thirty, he's interested in speed. What can you do for him right now? He's Internet smart and very sophisticated. Keep the age factor in mind.

More Closing Questions

Here are some low-pressure closes you can use.

"To get started, I just need your approval."

"When do you want to have this up and running or delivered?"

"How soon would you like to start increasing your sales, or saving time, or expanding?"

"Any reason why we can't get started?"

Assure Them

If the person's interested in what you have, but they're hesitating, say,

"I know exactly what you're saying. Most of our customers in your same situation have felt the same way, but once they got started, they said it was one of the best decisions they ever made for their company. Let's go ahead with this, I promise you won't regret it, ok? "

This is an assurance close. The person just needs a little nudge.

Another Alternate-Choice Close

Another good alternative choice phrase to use is, **"Which would be better for you? "**

When I'm ready to ship one of my On-Hold Programs, I say,

"Ralph, do you want to have us C.O.D. it, or put it on your credit card? Which would be better for you?"

It's a nice alternative choice close.

Find Out Why

If someone tells you they still want to think it over, say,

"In what areas are you still not convinced?"

This is a polite way of asking them why they're not going to buy your product.

Dealing With Cancellations

Can you remember the last time you got a cancel? People who never get a cancel are people who are afraid to take risks and ask for the order. Cancellations are a part of sales, and nobody likes them. If you're getting a **lot** of cancels, then you're probably slamming people or not finalizing the details. In the event you do get a cancel, say, *"Bob, apparently something specific made you unsure of our agreement. Tell me, what's bothering you?"*

This will salvage some of your cancels.

Find Out if They are the Buyer By Closing

If you're not sure if the person you're talking to is the decision maker, ask them for the order. Real decision makers won't have to talk to anyone. (Even if they tell you they do)

When They Want to Think it Over

Next time someone tells you they want to think about it, say,

> **"Tom, suppose you went ahead with this today. What's the absolute worst thing that could happen?"**

If he gives you some ridiculous reason like the building may burn down, say,

> **"Do you really think that could happen?"**

This technique gets them to think more rationally.

Determine What They're Shopping For

If your prospect wants to shop around, say,

> **"What specifically will you be looking for in another company that you feel we're not able to give you? Do you know what company you'll be comparing us too?"**

If they tell you they don't know, they're not a prospect. You can also tell them that during the next few days while you're processing their order, if they can find a better offer/price, fax it to you and you'll match it. If they won't agree to that, they're not shopping around, they're getting rid of you, move on.

A similar stall is, "I want to think about it." Say,

"If you were to make the decision right now, do you feel you have enough information from me to do that?

If yes, ask,

"And what would that decision be?"

If he says no, ask,

"What else would you need to know?"

We're just trying to get the person to open up and find his real objection.

Run the Numbers With Them

If you have to review a lot of numbers with someone, ask them if they have a calculator and have them go through the numbers with you. This gets them involved.

14

Last Resort Closing Techniques

Despite your best efforts, sometimes they still don't buy. Here are some last resort closing ideas.

Be the Next in Line

If you lose business to another competitor, position yourself so you're the next in line to do business with. For example,

"Frank, if things don't work out, or your new supplier is out of stock on an item you need, will you call me?"

This at least plants a seed. Occasionally they will call you.

Find Out Why They're Not Interested

A good question to ask someone who says they're not interested in your offer is,

"Jim, is it because you just don't have the time to do this right now, or are you really just not interested in this type of product/service?"

Many times it's just a bad time for them. Ask them about following up.

Hand It Off

Here's a technique called the "hand-off." It's very effective and can close some of the sales you might have lost. When a customer's sitting on the fence or undecided, have someone else call them to ask them why they're not buying. It's good to use someone who's a salesperson. You'll find that a different voice or point of view can swing the sale in your favor. You should compensate the other salesperson if they save the sale.

Would They EVER Buy?

If you know you're not going to get the sale, ask the prospect if they could ever see themselves using your product or service in the future. If they say yes, ask them what would have to change? They may tell you the real reason they're not buying.

Get Permission to Call Back

If you've been working with someone and find that you're not going to do business at this time, ask if it would be alright for you to call back in three months. Most will say OK. Call that person back every three months for a full year. If after one year they haven't bought, they most likely won't. By doing this, you would have called throughout all their seasons and quarters. Keep in mind, you don't want to have a million callbacks. Each time you call, review what you spoke about and ask for the order.

Ask About Other Products

If you offer several types of products and someone turns you down on one, you may want to mention some of the others. If a person I've been calling tells me they won't be doing business with me, I might say, "Do you advertise on radio or do you go to trade shows?" If they answer yes to one of those questions, I tell them that we also produce radio commercials and audio business cards. (Audio business cards are on a cassette that gives your customer a six-minute presentation about your company). Sometimes you'll find they're interested in these other products. If nothing else, at least they know you have other products if the need ever arises.

Take a Risk

Top producers always take chances and ask for the order. To be good at sales, you need to become a risk taker. Be willing to try to close every sale! When I lose a sale, before hanging up I say

> **"Jim, are you sure the decision you're making is in the best interest of your company?"**

I've got nothing to lose, and some people will call back a few days later after thinking about it more.

Have Them Put You Into Their File

If you lose your business to another vendor, ask them to put the info you sent them in the same file with the other company's. Every time they open the file they'll see your name. If their supplier is out of something, or they go out of business, they may just call you. If a new manager comes aboard, he may call you to find out what you're offering. Pretty slick, eh?

It's Direct, But it Works

Here's a brutal statement to say to someone who tells you it can't fit into their budget.

> **"Frank, the $400 comes out to just $7.70 a week to have this. Is your company in that bad a financial situation?"**

It's to the point, but you have to realize the budget excuse is normally a stall. If I know I'm talking to a large company, I'll use the above statement. If I'm talking to a Mom and Pop company, I'll try to work out terms. Since I call on companies that are making millions of dollars in annual sales, I know they can afford it.

Get a Decision

We all have those customers that just keep hesitating or still want to think about it. The best approach for these people is the direct one. Say,

> **"Jim, we've been talking about this for a month now. You know everything there is to know about this to make a decision, and if you weren't interested, we would have stopped talking long ago. So let's go ahead with this, ok?"**

This will definitely let you know where you stand. Since you don't have anything to lose in the first place, ask for the order!

15

The Price Issue

If you're a salesperson, you most likely have people asking you for a lower price, or telling you your price is too high, regardless of how high or low it is. This section will help you close more of those sales without giving away your profits.

Trade for Testimonials

If you have to lower your price to make the sale, tell them once they get your product/service and they're happy with it, get them to agree to sending you a short note on their letterhead stating they're happy with your product/service. Testimonial letters really help close sales.

Break it Down

Break down the price over the course of a month, week, year, or more.

> **"Yes, it is three hundred dollars, but that comes out to less than a dollar a day. I know you're not in such dire straits that your budget couldn't handle a dollar a day, are you?"**

This is a little rough, I agree. I'd only use it on someone whom you feel is stringing you along. You could leave off the dire straits part to soften it up a little bit. You just want to get the point across that it's not that expensive over the long haul.

Be Blunt

If a customer wants to chew you down on price and you know it's ridiculously low, say,

> **"Jim, in your industry I'm sure there are people who sell your product/service for less. Would you personally buy the cheapest product on the market in your industry?**
>
> **Or, "Jim, if you want the lowest price on the market, then you'll have to sacrifice one of**

three things: Quality, service, or results. Which
one of these are you willing to give up?"

Let them know buying cheap is going to cost them in the
long run.

How to Say the Price

Whenever mentioning price you should cushion it a little.

"It's only $295 and that comes with a three-year
warranty."

"It's only $395 and most of our customers tell
us they make their investment back the first
month."

Be aware when mentioning the price. I normally say "two
hundred and seventy-five dollars" first. If I just say "two seventy-five," some jokers think two dollars and seventy-five cents.
Once I tell them the price the first time, I then say "two sev-
enty-"five. They now know I'm talking in the hundreds.

Whenever mentioning a competitors price and you have
it beat, say your price is "only two seventy-five." Say the
competitor's price as "two hundred and ninety-five dollars."
Say it long and say it slow. Make their price seem soooooooooo
big.

Don't Drop—Add

Instead of deducting price, try adding a product. It's usually less expensive than deducting $100 from the price. If you
have to deduct price, instead of speaking in cash terms, speak
in percentages. Instead of saying you can deduct $100, say
that you can give them 10% off. Psychologically it sounds like
a lot more, when in reality it could be much less.

Get Their Price First

If your prospect tells you he has a bid from another company, try and find out what the price is. If you can beat it, you
may get the business immediately. I simply say,

"Louie, what price did they quote you?"

Also keep in mind they may be using this as a ploy. If you
give your price first, they'll say the price they got was lower.
I tell them to fax me the proposal and I'll take it to my man-

ager to see what I can do. If they don't send it, I know they're bluffing. Get their price first, it puts you in the driver's seat.

Questions to Weed Out the Nonbuyers

Here's a very direct question. Sometimes I say to a customer,

> **"The price is $400. Is that something that can fit into your budget, or are we finished talking?"**

If they continue talking, they're interested. It really weeds out the buyers from the non-buyers. I generally use this for the person who wants the price right up front. I'll normally give the price, and ask

> **"Now, would you like to know what you'd get for that? "**

If they won't even let me justify the price, I move on. And I don't send info!

Use Comparisons to Minimize Price

I like to use this phrase,

> **"Jim, this is a fantastic price. You're getting a Rolls Royce for the price of a Volkswagen. Let's go ahead with it, ok?"**

Present the Price Difference, Not the Total

Whenever talking about a difference in price, only talk about the amount difference. For example, the customer tells you that $2000 is too high, and tells you he can get it for $1,900. Instead of talking about the $2000 price, just say to the prospect,

> **"So what you're saying is that the only thing that's keeping us from doing business is 100 dollars. Is that right?"**

If he says yes, and you can meet his price, say,

> **"Jim, If I can get you that same price, are you ready to do business today, or are we finished talking?"**

If he tells you he still has to think about it, tell him the owner will give him the same price if he's willing to do business right now. If he stalls on that, thank him for his time and hang up. If he's serious, he'll give you the business.

Start High

When you give someone the price of your product/service, you may want to give them the quote on your most expensive package. Of course only a few people will go for it. It's easier to work your way down on price. This technique will insure you never miss those big whales. Your sales will increase because over the long term your sales average will be much higher.

Trade Concessions

If you absolutely have to drop price, make it a policy that the person will have to give you their order right now. This is a trade off, not a gift! If they won't abide by their own terms, you don't want that type of customer. Thank-you and good-bye.

More Price Lines

Here's something you may want to try when mentioning price.

> **"Tom, if you sold just one case of these, you'd show a profit of 300%. The price is just a simple investment of $100."**

> Or, **"Tom, you're in the collision repair industry. If you made just one sale from this, it would pay for itself many times over."**

> Or, **"It's just a simple one-time investment of only $400 and you own it outright."**

You can develop phrases similar to these. You can use them right before or after you give the price.

Create Doubt About a Lower Price

Try putting doubt in your customers mind. If a prospect tells you they can get your product cheaper from a competitor, try,

> **"I'm surprised to hear that. We've been in business 10 years, and our customers tell us we have some of the best prices in the industry. The price**

they are quoting you is so low, I find it hard to believe that they could make a profit."

You then should review what you're giving them, and compare it point for point with the competitor's. If they do have a better price for the same product, say,

"Do you know how long they've been in business?"

This gets the prospect thinking that maybe the price he's getting is too good. He'll start wondering if the company will be around a year from now.

Ask About the Downside of Buying on Price

Sometimes people are so price conscious they'll buy a cheaper model just to save $50. Many times people tell me they can get one of my On-Hold Message systems on cassette for $50 less. I know cassettes wear out and break and that they'll be very unhappy with the purchase. I'll say things like,

"Have you thought through the disadvantages of using cassettes that wear out and break every two weeks, versus a state of the art compact disc that never wears out or breaks, and comes with a lifetime guarantee?"

Or just a simple phrase such as,

"Have you thought through the downside of that decision?"

Sure it's direct, but what have you got to lose? They just told you they weren't buying.

Don't Agree With the Price Shopper

Make sure when talking about price you never agree with someone if they say your price is too high. Don't say things like *"I agree," "I think our prices are high, too."* Or, *"Yeah, prices seem to keep going up."* I'm amazed at how many people actually say these things. Never justify your price. Add value instead.

Point Out the Cost of Doing it Themselves

Explain to people how much time or how much it would cost them if they tried to do what you offer on their own. Some people tell me they can produce their own On-Hold Program. I say,

> "Jim, it's going to take you 20-30 hours to write the scripts. You'll then have to rent space at a music studio, usually $200 an hour with a minimum of 4 hours. You'll have to interview announcers who charge $75 to $100 an hour, and you'll have to get the rights to your music copyrighted or you can be fined. If you do this on your own, it's going to cost you thousands. As busy as you are, can you really see yourself finding the time to do all that?"

As you can see, I help them realize all the time and work that's involved. If you're a realtor, you can modify this concept to explain everything someone would have to go through to sell a home on their own, and why it's in their best interest to use a professional.

Minimize the Price

Minimize the price to sell a higher priced item. Example:

> "Our basic package is $80. For $20 more you can get the deluxe package."

Notice I didn't say the deluxe package was $100. I only mentioned the small $20 price difference. If you were selling homes, you could say,

> "There's only a ten thousand dollar difference between this house and the other. Since you like this one better, it's only going to make your mortgage payment an extra 25 dollars a month. I suggest you take this one. You'll be a lot happier if you do, don't you agree?"

Ask How Long They Expect it to Last

If your prospect tells you he's going to buy a cheaper product, say,

> "How long do you plan on using it?"

> "How long do you plan to keep it?"

> "Were you looking for something on a temporary basis, or looking for something that would

last the life of your company?"

Equate cheap with short term and temporary.

A Question to Ask

Here's an interesting thing to say to someone who says they can get a lower price from someone else.

> **"Susan, we know some of our competition sells this for less. They know best what their product/service is worth. Do you plan on using this long term or short term?"**

This gets them thinking if buying cheap is worth it to them. Ask them what type of results they're trying to achieve. Point out the problem they may have when trying to meet their goals with a cheaper product/service.

Ask When They'll Have the Funds

If somebody says they don't have the money, say,

> **"When do you think you'll have the money?"**

If they say they can't afford it, ask,

> **"When do you think you'll be able to afford it?"**

Remember, before you can answer an objection, you have to know why they're saying it.

Price Objection Responses

Here are a couple of things to say when they tell you your price is too high.

> **"The price may seem high to you now, but this one time investment is going to last the life of your company."**

> **" The price may seem high now, but think of all the years of enjoyment you'll be getting from it."**

> **"The price may seem high now, but think of the return you'll be getting back on your investment."**

Differentiate Yourself

If your product/service is being compared with another company that has an equal price, you have to convince the prospect on what makes your company different, or why it will make a difference to him to choose you. Quicker deliveries, being open on weekends, open invoice, etc. Look around and find things in your company that it does well, or that most companies in your industry don't do. Use that to your advantage. Differentiate yourself.

Use Humor
Here's a response that generally gets a good laugh. Often when I tell a customer the price is 400 dollars, they'll ask me to give them a good price. I pause for a moment and say,

"I can let you have it for 500 hundred."

They respond by saying you just told me it was 400 hundred! I say,

"Yeah I know, but you said you wanted a GOOD price. That is a GOOD price! The 400 hundred was a GREAT price!"

There's no rule that says you can't have fun on the phone.

Another Objection Response
If they say it costs too much or is not in the budget, respond with,

"Are you saying that because you think the price is beyond your budget, or are you saying that because you don't think you'll get a return back on your investment?"

This statement will help weed out the real objection why they're not going to buy.

When They Want the Price First ...
Sometimes people jump right on you and want the price. Since I sell Telephone On-Hold Messages, I say,

"The price varies depending on your phone system. Jim, do you know if you have a phone system that can play music through your phone lines?"

Since this is a logical question, he'll answer it. Once he

tells me, I continue my presentation as I normally would.

Give the Price Based on Quantity

If you're selling cases of goods, you might say,

> **"The price varies depending on the quantity you order. In your situation, how many cases do you think you'd want?"**

Or,

> **"Jim, in order for me to give you the best possible price, I just need to know ..."**

Then go right into your presentation.

Discuss Payment Plans

If you have financing, or can work out a payment plan with a customer who wants your product, here's a good way to say it:

> **"You know Bill, I was talking with someone the other day who was in the same situation as you, and here's what he did ..."**

Then explain the payment plans to him. People like to hear how other people in their same situation solved a problem. It's human nature.

Point Out How Many to Get the Next Price Break

Instead of saying your price break is at $100, say,

> **"If you order just four more cases, you could have the price break. That would make it only $15 a case instead of $17. Would you like to take advantage of that?"**

A Personal Tip for Getting Discounts

Whenever purchasing products or services for yourself, always say to the salesperson,

> **"How much better can you do on the price?"**

Notice I didn't say, *"Can you do any better on the price?"* That's a yes or no question. The other way you say it makes the person have to justify the price. For many salespeople it's just easier to give the discount. If you're the owner of a company, make sure your purchasing agent uses this phrase. It can literally save you thousands of dollars. I use it all the time when I purchase just about anything. Even huge franchises will give you discounts. My wife says it all the time, and she's constantly amazed at the discounts she gets.

Make Money by Discounting Your Price

Here's a technique that can actually make you more money by discounting your price. Tell the customer you may be able to help him out on the price if he could help you. Tell him when he takes delivery of your product and is completely satisfied, can he give you a few referrals of people who he feels would like to receive information about your product or service. This does two things.

•It closes the sale right then if you can meet or negotiate a price.

•Some of the referrals he gives you may turn into sales.

16

Asking for Referrals

It's a lot easier to call someone you've been referred to, trust me. Here are some ideas for you.

When to Ask

A good time to ask for a referral is when a customer turns you down. He'll feel bad and want to make it up to you. Try not to walk away empty handed.

Ask After a Compliment

Anytime you help a customer solve a problem with great customer service, or they tell you your company is great, etc. Ask them for a referral.

Get an Association Directory

Ask good customers if they belong to an association of their industry. If yes, ask them how you can get a copy of the association book. Sometimes they'll tell you just to call up and order. Other times they'll say it costs $50 and you have to be a member. Ask the customer if you send him the $50 would he order one for you. Some will. If not, ask if they have last year's copy they can send you. This technique can literally get you hundreds or even thousands of names and numbers of decision makers. If they do not belong to an association, say:

> **"Do you have any family members or relatives who own a business that you think might like to get info on our product? It's a lot better to be specific than asking, "...who do you know?"**

Can you think of everyone you know in a split second? Of course not. Neither can they. So, make it easy. (You can also ask if they have anyone in their Rolodex.)

Get Specific Referrals

Ask for a specific referral. For example: if I sell a program to a boat dealership, I ask them for the contact name and number of their supplier. Every company does business with other companies. Who do your customers do business with? Ask them for that specific referral. Instead of being specific, you can be generic. Who does their security? Who cleans their office? Who do they buy their office supplies from? By asking for one specific referral, you'll get one most of the time.

No Referral? Get a Recommendation Letter

If they've purchased from you and are happy with your product/service, but don't have any referrals for you, ask them to send you a recommendation or success letter about your product or service. A good recommendation letter can do wonders for you.

Ask for Referrals Within the Company

Depending on what you're selling, (such as life insurance), ask the person if anyone else in the company would like to know about what you have to offer. If it's not a company, ask if anyone in their family would.

Ask Where They Worked Before

If you run across someone who tells you they just started at the company you're trying to sell to, ask them for the contact name of their former employer. Many times they'll tell you who to talk with, and if the other company was using your type of product or service.

Ask ANYONE You Know

Make sure family, friends, and relatives know what you sell. The average person knows about 250 people. It's hard to believe, but think of where you buy your gas, insurance, health spa, cleaners, doctors, etc. Everyone should know what you sell. Marketing experts believe that if you've been in business two years as an individual or a company, one million people should know who you are, and what you do. If only 1% of the people did business with you, you'd have made one thousand sales!

Ask for Referrals in a Letter

If your company doesn't have a referral letter, then make one up yourself. I send a referral letter with all shipments that go out. If that's not possible in your situation, you may have to mail it on your own. The small amount of money you spend on the postage will be well worth it. I usually send it with a self addressed stamped envelope. They can also call, e-mail, or fax me their referrals. My letter simply reads:

To: John Smith

From: Joe Catal

I'd like to ask you a personal favor. As you know, all business people like myself depend on referrals. If you have anyone in your business Rolodex that you think would like to receive information about our service, can you please send me their names and numbers? For anyone who purchases our product, I'll send you $25.

Thank You!

You can also ask if they have any brothers, sisters, or relatives whom they think might like to receive information on your service. If you sell to businesses, you can list examples of industries at the bottom of the page to help jolt their memory. And as I said earlier, you can ask for a specific referral.

Keep in mind, by asking for referrals, you'll not only get new business, but also find new industries you may not have thought of. In order for this to work, you must be persistent! Make sure you put a few lines on the form so they can write the names and numbers in. No matter what type of product or service you sell, you can use this format to develop a referral letter. Also keep in mind, people know other people in their industry. If you sell to marketing directors at resorts you can ask them for names of other marketing directors they know. You should also compensate people if a referral they send you turns into a sale. I've found it takes about thirty days before you start seeing results. I guarantee you'll generate extra business from this.

Always Be Professional

Being professional with your customers will give you opportunities ordinary salespeople miss. The reality is, customers are concerned with who they give referrals out to. They simply won't open the door for you if you're less than professional. You ever notice how some people seem to get referrals on a regular basis, and others can't remember when the last time was they got one? A professional image with great customer service = referrals.

17

Sending Info

A disadvantage we have when selling by phone is the visual one ... they're there, and we're here. Therefore, it can be beneficial to get the visual aspect of communication involved. Here are some time-tested tips that work for me.

Just the Fax

If you have info you fax on a regular basis, highlight it with a dark magic marker for certain key points. Always write with a black medium point magic marker to fax, and print, don't write! You can also use the self-adhesive laminates to keep your info always in good condition. You can get them at any office supply store. Yes, they'll fax through.

Don't Use an Ordinary Fax Cover Sheet

There are humorous books out that can be used as fax material. Your fax cover sheet doesn't have to be boring! Make it stand out. I send all types of funny faxes. Don't send anything offensive. Look through your bookstore or go to an online bookstore and type in "fax cover sheets"and you'll see books already made up with fax cartoons and funny drawings. Just make some copies of the ones that pertain to your situation and use them. Show your prospect you're different from the run of the mill salespeople. If you don't want to use humorous faxes, make sure your fax cover sheet explains what you do. Don't use an ordinary fax coversheet. Those generic ones you buy at the store or get with your fax software are boring and useless.

Your fax cover sheet should be like a business card.

Look for Articles to Send

Be sure to scan the Internet, papers, and magazines for articles written about your type of product or service. Include these articles in the info you send to people. People like to know that other people have had good success with your type of product or service, plus, people tend to believe more of what they read than what they hear. That's why those gossip newspapers sell so much!

Call Back After Sending the Fax

Whenever sending a fax, always call back to make sure the person received it. This will avoid the "I never received your info," I tell the person who answers the phone that I just sent a three page fax to Jim that he's expecting. Can you make sure he gets that on his desk for me? Don't assume that because your fax machine showed it went through that they got it. If it's a big company, the papers can get mixed in with all the others. It's not easy being a superstar. It takes hard work to do the little things low producers don't want to do.

Fax to the Other Influencer

Sometimes when you call someone back after faxing them info you find out they haven't run it by their office manager or other influential decision maker. Here's a way to avoid that. After you fax your contact, call back and ask for the name of the other decision maker. The *next day* fax the same package to them. Write a note telling them that John (your contact) will be talking to you about our product. Tell them that if they have any questions to call you personally. Many times the owner hasn't even told the manager about it. The manager will then go to the owner and bring it up! They'll actually have a one-on-one meeting about it. If they're interested, the manager (influential decision maker) will more than likely call you. Once he's convinced, you have a great chance of getting the deal. This technique may also get you to bypass the "committee meeting" stall, and speed the sales process up. It's very effective.

Send Names

If you've done business with a large recognizable name company, tell people about it. A lot of people will think if they went with you, you must be all right. Send the names of those companies with the info you send out. Also, if someone says they want to run it by their marketing department, you can say:

"Jim, some of the largest companies in the industry such as ABC Corp. have already done all the research for you. They found that we were the best company to go with."

In essence what you're saying is that the best experts in the industry agree that you're the best to go with. It lets the prospect realize he can't compete with that type of expertise, and it may not be necessary to ask his own people, if he really does in fact have a marketing dept.

Have Them Send You Stuff

Get the prospect to send *you* information. If a prospect wants you to send info, you can also ask them to fax you info on their company so you'll be better prepared to discuss their needs when you call back. If they fax you, you have a pretty good prospect.

Send Info ONLY for a Reason

If you have to send info, say,

"From what I've explained to you today, along with the info you'll be getting, if we check out and everything else is to your liking, what happens next? "

Or, **"From what I've explained to you today, along with the info you'll be getting, if we check out and everything is to your liking, would there be anything you can think of that would keep you from going ahead with this?"**

They should say they'll buy. If not, find out why you're sending the info in the first place.

Go Online With Them

If they're at their desk and have a computer, you can ask them to bring up your company web site. It makes a great brochure, and you can use this as an angle for the send info stall.

If you don't have a computer at your desk to review it with them, download the pages and put them in a binder so you have a copy of your website in front of you. you can also use them as fax pages.

If you have to go on a face-to-face presentation, and the people have access to the Internet show them your company website. It adds more credibility. And if there are testimonials, ask them to click on them.

Mark Up Your Literature

When sending info to someone, don't be afraid to mark it up. Circle important points. Have an arrow pointing at a certain paragraph that says, read this! This will actually get a lot of people to look at those points.

P.S.

Whenever sending info to someone, always put a P.S. on it. People always read a P.S. Put a powerful point about your product /service there.

Send it Right Now

If you need to fax or e-mail someone information, you should do it as quickly as possible. If they get your information right away, this will make a good first impression about your service.

Also, send info immediately after making a sale on a cold call. It should be there in five minutes. Do it before you write up the order. If a person just gave you a credit card, you want to relieve his anxiety that he wasn't ripped off. When he sees that fax come through, he'll have something tangible in his hand. This is letting him know you're for real, and don't play games. At the end of a sale, always let your customers know you'll be sending info out on your company right away, and to check their fax machine or e-mail in fifteen minutes.

Qualify Before Sending Info

If you have to go through someone to get to the decision maker, here's a good question to ask if they want you to send info.

"If you like what you see, would it be possible for me to talk with the members of the committee?

Or, **"...talk with the owner, partner etc."**

If they say no, you have to find out how they make buying decisions. Studies have shown that the average decision maker spends between 9 and 20 SECONDS reviewing written sales material such as faxes or brochures. Don't just send info to send info.

Send Self-Promotion

Have you ever considered promoting yourself? Some phone reps write a one page summary of who they are, who some of their big name customers are, how long they've been with the company or working in the customer's industry, etc. Since I wrote this book, I started sending a one-page summary about that. I know it gives the extra credibility I need to beat out my competition. Not only that, I'm marketing my book. If they don't do business with me, they might just buy the book. Use all the weapons you have. Don't be afraid to promote yourself. Many reps like to start their letters with a mission statement. Some reps put their photo on it.

Ask Why They Haven't Done Anything Yet

If you're talking to someone who says they've had other companies send them info on your type of product/service, ask them why they haven't gone ahead and purchased it. I say,

> **"With all the info you've been collecting about this, why haven't you've done anything yet?"**

There has to be a reason why they're collecting all that info and not buying. If they tell me to send info, I say, "

> **"With all the info you already have, you know all there is to make an informed decision about this. Why not just get started today?"**

The reality is, they probably will never buy your product or service. Ask for the order and move on. If he insists he wants info, let's get tough:

> **"Jack, if I send you the info, when will you have had enough time to review it?"**

If he says a week, say,

> **"When I call you back, I'm going to ask for your**

order. **If you haven't chosen one of the other companies, will you definitely give me your order, or are you going to keep putting this off?"**

I can assure you, once you confront the info junkie with a yes or no decision to buy, he'll run like a scared rabbit. Don't play games with these non-buyers. Put them against the wall, and pull the trigger.

Fax Back a Summary

After a conversation with someone, you should send them a fax on what you spoke about and what you agreed to do. It keeps everyone on the same page. Don't trust your memory, or anyone else's when it comes to business transactions.

It's even better if you can fax it to them, and have them initial it and fax it back. This may only be applicable in special situations. I normally do this when the decision maker delegates me to someone else. Once I get all the info to get started from the manager, I fax the agreement to the decision maker and have him ok it. I don't have the manager ok it, I want the decision maker to see it. I've been burned enough to know many times the owner will pass you off just to get rid of you. The manager who wants to act like Mr. Big will lead you on. Once it's time to pay up for the work done, they tell you the owner shot it down. Get the approval from the top. Once he has to put his signature on a contract, he'll call to cancel if he was bluffing. If he wasn't blowing you off, he'll approve it.

Get a Time

If you have to send info and can't set a specific time or day to call back, say,

"When do you think you'll have a chance to go through the information so we can speak again?"

In the real world of selling, if someone can't even give you a specific day to call back, I wouldn't take them too seriously. If they tell you they'll call you when they get a chance, don't send it.

Note: Over the years I've learned if I have to send info, and the person won't schedule a call back, and tells me he'll call if they're interested, it's not worth it. Don't send info to these types of people.

18

Dealing With Common Objections

In this section I'll address many of the common objections most of us hear on the phone.

"I Want to Think it Over"

Whether you realize it or not, when a customer tells you he wants to think it over, this is a great opportunity for you to close the sale. The only time a customer ever says that is after you have given your full presentation. As we all know, that's the best time to close the sale. If you sell on the phone or face-to-face, you know the reality of call backs. The chance of closing the sale decreases dramatically. From now on you'll know exactly how to respond and ask for the order. I've written it out for any type of product or service.

For example, with the telephone on-hold messages I sell, when the prospect says he wants to think it over, I respond with,

> **"Dan, are you saying that because you want to think about what you want to put on the program, or are you saying that because you think the price is too high?"**

Most will say the price is too high. If they say that, simply reply back,

> **"How much too high do you think it is?"**

If they say $100, (and I can meet or negotiate a better price), I'll say,

> **"Other than the price, is there anything else that would keep you from going ahead with this?"**

Most will say no. If you can meet or negotiate a better price, tell the prospect you can, and immediately write up the sale.

Other Examples:

"Are you saying that because you want to think about how many cases you want to order, or are you saying that because you think the price is too high?"

"Are you saying that because you want to think about how often you'll use our service, or are you saying that because you think the price is too high?"

As you can see, this will work for any product or service. You'll be surprised how effective this routine is. After asking this question, you'll know exactly where you stand. Always keep in mind, before you can answer an objection, you have to ask a question back to find out why they're saying it. You simply just can't blurt out some scripted response such as,

"What is it you want to think about?"

"I'm your best source of information, what do you need to know?"

"You know all there is to know, what do you want to think about?"

These are all old and stale techniques that get you nowhere fast. We all know the main objection is money. Get the money objection out on the table and deal with it now! You'll close a lot more sales.

"Can You Give Me a Better Price?"

When people ask me for a better price, I say,

"Jim, we do have a better price. Right now you're getting one program for $400. You can get three programs for $795. That would make it only $265 a program. Should we sign you up for that program? "

Or. "Would you like to take advantage of that?"

I've found 5-10 percent of the people will say yes. Most of the others will just say they'll stick with what they're getting.

"I Only Do Business Locally"

"Jim, I wouldn't be calling you long distance if I thought you could get this product/service locally at the price(s) we offer. Since I have you on the line, let me tell you what the price(s) would be for you. If you'd like to know more, I'll answer any of your questions, if not, I promise, I'll let you get right back to work. Fair enough?"

Of course you'll have to have some numbers ready. Also, if you sell something that's not possible to give an exact price on, use ballpark figures, hourly rates, yearly rates, etc.

In the real world of selling to this type of customer you'll have to send him info. He probably doesn't do business long distance because he's been burned in the past and doesn't trust anybody, or he simply doesn't want to go through the hassle of changing vendors. Assuming I can do better on price or some other area, and may have an opportunity of getting my foot in the door, I always send my literature with a few extra items. I include a copy of our company license, Dunn & Bradstreet number, Better Business Bureau letter, a list of any associations we are a supplier of, and three referrals of people who do business with us in his city or state. If you have people in his same industry using your product/service, send those referrals if it's ok with the customer. This shows your prospect credibility and the legitimacy of your company. This will eliminate the, "I don't know your company routine."

If a customer ever says he doesn't know your company, say,

"What would you need to know about us to make you feel comfortable in doing business with us? "

Usually it's some of the above items I listed. Once I started sending that info automatically, it took care of that objection. When you call them back and they say they've checked you out and everything looked good, ask for the order/appointment. If you call back and they tell you they still haven't checked you out, schedule another call back. If you call back and hear the same excuse, move on, they're not a buyer. For the customer who does check you out, work with him on his terms best as you can. Give a little leeway to bring a new account in. A little discount now, will pay for itself in the long run. If he only wants to order one case and your minimum is two, send him one! If you have a service that has to be used a minimum of three months, but someone only wants to try it for thirty days, do it if you can. A small slice of the pie now, can turn into the whole pie in the future. Just keep in mind that these types of sales need a lot of nurturing and attention at the beginning. If Jim calls and says his other supplier is out of something and you have it, ship it to him as fast as possible. Show him how fast your service is compared to what he's now using.

"I Have a Partner"

As we all know, prospects will tell you to send info to get rid of you. Here's something they're saying that's being used the same way. "I have a partner." During a two-month period I kept records of 57 prospects who told me they had a partner. The next day I called the company back and said to whoever picked up the phone,

"Hi. Jim asked me to send him some information on our company. How do you spell his last name?"

After getting the name I said,

"Is Jim the only owner of the company, or does he have a partner?"

Twenty-two of the 57 people told me there was no partner! What's amazing is that when I called them back to ask for the order, not one of them made a purchase! They all said the partner turned it down. Out of the 35 that did have partners, only nine of them let me speak with the other partner. Out of those nine, five made a purchase. Out of the remaining 26 that did not let me speak with their partner, only one made a purchase. I've come to the conclusion that this is another stall that's as popular as the send info routine.

When they say they have to run it by their partner, say,

"Jim, is your partner in?"

If yes, say,

> **"Could you see if he has a moment to talk to me. I'd just like to run this by him and answer any of his questions. This way the both of you can make an informed decision about this."**

If he tells you his partner's busy, say,

> **"What time later today would be a good time for me to call back and talk with him?"**

If he gives you a time, great. However, don't be surprised if the prospect gets very short with you and says, "You don't need to call him back. Just send me your info and if we're interested we'll call you." There's the red flag. Ask him if he has access to the Internet, (most do). Give him your name, number and web site address. Tell him,

> **"Check our web site out because it has everything you need to know about us. If your partner's interested, give me a call back and we can discuss this further."**

Since I've been using this technique, very few people have called back. However, the ones that let me speak with their partner, I've been closing almost 50% of these!

If you don't have a website, leave him your name and number and tell him if his partner is interested to give you a call. Then if he is interested, you'll send out an information package.

Also, if you do talk with the partner, a lot of times he and the owner will be in the office together. Ask him to put you on a speaker phone. You'll find that many times doing this you'll get the order, or they'll say they do have interest and send info. This is legitimate! Set a day and time to call back. Also, if they're not interested, they'll tell you. It saves a lot of time. Sometimes you'll run into a situation where a committee is involved. I ask if I can call during the meeting to tell them about this. Sometimes they'll say yes, most of the time it's a no. I ask if he'd like to call me during the meeting. Again, some will, most won't. On this you'll have to use your gut feeling. Is the person your talking to for or against your product? Will they recommend it? What's the benefit they see? I also ask if the committee likes this, what would be the next step.

You have to go into the partner stall with an "I'm going to call your bluff attitude." From now on whenever someone tells you they have a partner, keep in mind almost 50% don't!

Also, depending on what you're selling, you may not want to present to the single partner at all, but set up a convenient time when all parties involved would be in. If they tell you their partner's in a different location, try to set up a conference call or get the number to the other location and call him.

"Send Information"

Here are a few ideas of mine, along with some by Art Sobczak. I know you'll find something here you can use.

Depending on the product or service you sell, you may or may not have to send information to your customer. You need to have the mindset that every person you talk to will ask you to send information. People have been using this stall forever. The hardest thing about this objection is determining how you weed out the real prospects from the ones who just want to get rid of you. Here are a couple of things I've learned over the years.

Understand now, that this is my opinion based on my personal experience. As a general rule, I've found that men will use the "send info" ploy as a way to get rid of salespeople. Women who ask that info be sent are more likely to be interested in reviewing it and running it by other people. Whenever I'm speaking with a woman, I know I'll have to send info. This is how I found women do business over the phone.

Here are some ideas that will help you weed out the non-buyers. Pay close attention to the questions they ask and how long you've been talking to them. Sending info to someone whose spent ten or fifteen minutes with you is a lot better prospect than someone who spent two.

"Jim, what type of information would be most important to you in order for you to make an informed decision about this?"

If he just tells you to send anything you have and he'll review it, this is not a good sign. You want him to ask for info on specific things. If he says he wants to look at your pricing structure, review it with him again.

"Jim, as soon as I finish taking your information down, I'll fax you everything you need to know about us, along with a list of references.

109

> If during the next week while we're processing your order, you're not happy with what our customers have to say about us, just call me back and I'll cancel your order personally. That's fair to you isn't it?"

Again, depending on what you're selling, this may or may not be applicable to your situation. Also, instead of references, you can also say,

> "I'll send you our Better Business Bureau information and our company license."

If all else fails and you have to send info, say,

> "Jim, from what I've explained to you today, along with the information you'll be getting, if we check out, and everything else is to your liking, would there be anything you can think of that would keep you from giving me your order the next time I call?"

This is an EXCELLENT question. You might hear responses about fitting it into their budget, having a partner, moving in a month, etc. Therefore, always ask this question so you can smoke out any objections today. If they tell you they don't know, or they'll have to wait and see, you need to find out why. I usually respond back with,

> "Jim, when someone tells me that, it's usually because of the price. Do you feel our price is too high? " As we know, price is usually the issue. If so, say,

> "How much too high do you think it is?"

If they say ten dollars or five-hundred and you can meet or negotiate a better price, ask,

> "Other than the price, would there be anything else that would keep you from going ahead with this?"

If you can give them the price, put them on hold for a minute, come back on and tell them you can do it, but because the price is so low, their order has to be in today. Here's another good question to ask.

> "Jim, I'd be more than happy to send you information. So I can get a better idea of what would be best to send, I just need to ask you a few

110

questions."

If he doesn't have time to answer your questions, he's not a prospect.

"I Want To Shop Around."

Often a customer may want your product or service, but they want to make sure they're getting a good deal. Here are several ideas you can use. Modify them to fit your specific needs.

> **"Jim, do you feel there's something we're not offering you that you think you can get elsewhere? "**

Or,

> **"Jim, if during the next few days while we're processing your order, if you really believe you can find a better price/product/service than ours, just fax me their proposal and we'll match it. That's fair to you, isn't it?"**

Or,

> **"Just fax me their proposal and I'll take it to my manager to see if we can do better. That's fair to you, isn't it? "**

Or,

> **"That'll work for you, wouldn't it?"**

Keep in mind, many people use the "shop around" technique as a way to avoid buying from you. If they're sincere, they'll take you up on the offer. Also, ask them if they know the name of the company they'll be comparing you to. Most people have no clue. They'll say things like, "I'll look through the phone book." If they do give you a name, you'll know what you're up against.

If they insist on shopping around, say,

> **"Jim, I understand, but would you do me one favor? If you do find a better price/offer than ours, before you put your order in, would you fax me a copy of their proposal. I'd like to take it to my manager to see if we can do better. Ok?"**

This technique feeds on greed. If they do find a better deal, they'll call you last to see if you can do better. If you can do better, you've got the deal.

Always say this before hanging up.

> **"So, if I understand you, this will be a priority for you, and if I don't hear back from you by next Wednesday with a better proposal, I'll assume you didn't find a better offer, and you'll give me your order. Is that correct?"**

I assure you, this will automatically weed out the real buyer from the non-buyer. If he's serious, he'll say he'll give you the order when you call back. If not, you'll hear, "Well, I don't know if I can get to it by then," or, "It's really not a priority." If he says that, he's not a serious prospect. I like it when they tell me they may not have time to shop around in the next week. I ask them when during the next thirty days will they have three to four hours extra to do that? This shows them it's really time-consuming.

If you're still getting resistance, say,

> **"Jim, I've been doing this for a long time, and I can tell when people are evasive with me, it's almost always a money related issue. It's the price, isn't it?"**

Most of the time it's the price. If not, they'll normally tell you the real reason.

You can also ask them if they'll be personally doing the shopping around, or if they'll be delegating it to someone else. If they tell you they're going to let the office manager handle it, make sure you talk to that person! Tell the owner that you want to make sure they're comparing apples to apples. If the owner doesn't let you through to the manager, it's a bluff. He's not a prospect. Any logical and serious prospect would let you do that. If you do get to talk with the person they're delegating you to, give a full presentation to the person. If the owner tells you he'll be personally doing the shopping around, say,

> *"Jim, I really appreciate that a busy person like yourself is going to take an extra two or three hours this week to work on this. Our customers tell us we have the lowest prices in the indus-*

try, and I hate to see you waste all that time to find that out. Are you sure you wouldn't like to go ahead with this today?"

As we all know, no business owner has an extra two or three hours a week. This technique will weed out the buyers from the non-buyers.

19

Call Backs

Often when you call back after an initial call you'll get objections. Whenever someone doesn't purchase from me, I always say.

> **"Was it the product/service itself that caused you to come to that conclusion, or was it something else? "**

Or,

> **"I'm surprised to hear that. The last time we spoke you sounded interested in this. What made you change your mind? "**

Most of the time it won't be your product, it will be the price. This question will save you a few deals, always use it when you get turned down.

When you have a prospect who wants to give you his order but he's always busy, here are a couple of things I've been using with good success. First, always try to set an appointment for a day and a specific time to call back. Sometimes, depending on the industry, that may be hard. Realtors are a good example. How do they know what will happen between now and next week? If you can't set a definite appointment, you might try calling from your home after hours. There's no law that states you can't make sales on your own time! Here are a few more good ideas. Ask,

> **"What do you suggest we do to speed up the process to make this happen?**

Or, one of my personal favorites,

> **"Is there someone else you can delegate this to?"**

Many times they'll say yes! Remember, as a salesperson you have to think in terms of solutions. Sometimes they tell you they're leaving on an appointment or have to take a drive somewhere. Ask them if you could call them on their cell phone. Often they'll tell you that's a good idea.

What if a customer tells you he likes your product or service, but he's not really sure he wants to go ahead with it?

Say,

> **"Jim, normally when someone says that to me, it's almost always a money-related issue. Other than the price, is there anything else that's keeping you from going ahead with this?"**

Most of the time it will be the price, so try to work out a payment plan. Give them something extra, or lower your price if you can.

Sometimes when you call back, people will tell you they haven't read your literature or made a decision yet. I say,

> **"I understand, but are you just saying that to politely get rid of me, or do you have some questions I haven't answered to your full satisfaction yet?"**

The legitimate prospects will generally apologize and tell you to call them back within the week. Others will just tell you they don't have the time and they'll call you when they get a chance. That means "no."

Always remember, before you can answer an objection, you have to know why they're saying it. Keep a 3 x 5 card on your desk with these words.

Who, what, where, when, how, why, and if.

Before answering their objection, make sure you ask them a question back that starts with one of these words. Be careful of the tone of your voice when saying "why." It can come off as sounding adversarial.

To have good call backs, you really need to qualify your prospects well.

Call Back Script

Here's something I use.

> "Hello _____. This is _____ _____with ABC Company.I spoke to you yesterday/last week about the radio advertising. You told me you were interested in expanding your market share and asked me to call you back today.
>
> Real briefly, I just want to review what we spoke about.
>
> You said your company's going national and a radio campaign would really give it the jump start you need. We'll produce six one-minute spots. Each spot would include a jingle so callers will automatically recognize your company. We'll write the spots first. We'll then fax them over to you to review and make changes. Once you do that, we'll produce them and let you hear them. Once you ok it, we'll send them to you on the format of your choice. The total investment is only $4,000.
>
> Now are there any questions I can answer for you before I take your information down?"

Or,

> "Now is there anything you're still not sure about?"

Notice how we automatically called back and asked for the order. We didn't ask if they received our info or had a chance to talk to their partner.

We're not calling back to *"touch base,"* or *"wondering if you had a chance to review the info."* That's weak.

Design a call back script with the above format. You'll be surprised how many people give you the order. Remember the powerful statement,

> "Now are there any questions I can answer for you before I take your information down? "

The minute they say no, just write up the order! Don't discuss anything else. Don't blab about how they made a great decision, etc. You can thank them right before you hang up the phone. Go through your order form quickly, and don't stop unless they have a question. Don't come to a point on your form and start telling them how great this one point or feature will be for them. Maybe that's not even the point or feature they're sold on. If they do mention a point that they like, just agree with them. Make a short comment on how other customers say the same thing and move on.

Be time conscious when taking an order. You don't want them to tell you to call back because an important call came in. Remember, they're on an agenda too.

Call Back Reminder

To be good at phone sales, you need to stand out from the rest of the crowd. The day before I'm going to call someone back, I always fax or e-mail them a reminder. (If you had a specific time to call you would also write that in.)

April 10, 2002
To: Jim Johnson
From: Joe Catal

Jim,
Just a reminder, you asked me to call you back regarding the computer software.
I'll be calling you, <u>Monday, April 15th.</u>
I look forward to speaking with you personally.
Thanks,

Joe
P.S. If you'd like to call *me* before then, please do.

"Call Back in A Couple of Months / Not in Budget"

Generally these two objections go hand in hand. When they tell you to call back in a couple of months, you need to know why you're calling back. Just simply ask,

> **"What would make that a better time for you?"**

Generally it's their budget. However, they may be moving, changing names, merging, etc. When they tell you it's not in the budget, say,

> **"Other than your budget, is there anything else that's keeping you from going ahead with this?"**

Or you could say, "

> **"So if I understand you correctly, you'd like to have this, and if it wasn't for your budget, you'd go ahead with this. Is that correct?"**

Most people will say yes, or they might say something like their manager really isn't for this. Bingo! You just found out the real reason they're not buying. If it is their budget, try to work out a payment plan.

Some people like to say,

> **"What have you done in other situations when you wanted something that you knew would be good for your business, but didn't have the money for. How did you get it?"**

This statement gets them thinking that there are other areas they can pull money from. If they happen to be moving or going through some changes, the only thing you can really do is convince them on why it's in their best interest not to wait. Here's an example I use when I sell my Telephone On-Hold Message programs. If they say they're moving, I say,

> **"Jim, That's why it would be a good idea to have this system now. During the next three months, people would hear that you're moving and have your new address. I'll produce a second program for you absolutely free, this way when you do move, you'll be ready to go. That would work for you, wouldn't it?"**

This is better than nothing. At least you're offering a solution and asking for the order again.

What if you do have to call back in a few months? Some-

118

times a company is so busy that they have an interest in your product, but you have to call again during their slow season. Ask them what months are they usually slow? This is important! You'll want to make sure they'll have the funds. You don't want to call back and hear "It's our slow season, call us in a couple of months when things pick up." I always respond back with,

"Since it will be your slow season, what do I have to do now, to make sure I'm included in your budget? I'd hate to call back and be told it's your slow season, and you don't have the money."

This is a killer question! They might say they need to have a proposal in now in order to get it approved or reviewed for the upcoming budget. The person may also say that they'll have the money and that won't be a problem. If that's the case, then fine. When someone tells me to call back at a future date, I fax them a reminder letter the month before I'll be calling. I may even do this two months ahead of time if it's a big account I'm going after. This technique can also be used in the reverse way. If it's their slow season, you'll want to know when they'll be busy and have the money.

Call Back Strategies & Tips

❏ Tell people to write in their calendar when you'll be calling back. If you had to send them info and they haven't read it, this will remind them to look through it before you call.

❏ Keep in mind, you're either moving *toward* a sale, or *away* from it. It's never standing still. If you call a customer back and they still haven't read your info, you're moving away from the sale. Keep it moving closer, or move it out.

❏ Always take notes during your call. You can't remember everything someone tells you, plus when you call back, it impresses the customer when you can remember what you spoke about a week later.

❏ Tell them when you call back that you'll be asking for the order. Ask them if there would be anything that would keep them from giving you a decision when you call back. If they can't give you a definite yes or no, they're keeping something from you, partner, spouse, etc.

❑ If you call a prospect back and they don't seem that enthused or interested, say,

"Jim, the last time we spoke you thought this could really be a benefit to you. What happened since then?"

Maybe you'll find they had a partner who shot it down.

❑ We all have those prospects that tell us it's a deal and to call back next week to get started. Immediately say,

"Frank, between now and next week, could you see anything that would possibly hold this up?"

If he says no, say,

"What's keeping you from getting started today?"

Most will say they don't have the time. I respond with,

"Is their someone you can delegate this to, so we can get started?"

If he says no to that, don't put too much into the call back, unless the decision maker is the only person who can work with you. I suggest you learn this technique word-for-word.

❑ Are you chasing non-buyers? Every product or service on the market has a time limit in which they're sold. Example: I know that selling Telephone On-Hold systems is normally a two-call close. If I call someone back and they still haven't read my info or talked to their partner, I give them just one more call. After that, they can call me. (They very seldom do). How many calls does it take to close your product/service? If you have call backs way beyond your limit, call them back and just ask them point-blank why they're not doing business with you. Move them in or move them out. Make one last call to ask for the order. A good incentive that will help you close some of these deals, would be for you to make one last call and offer them a discount or throw in something extra. If they don't go for that, move on.

❏ If you have to call someone back, try to call back within 48 hours. If you talk to them within that period of time, they'll retain about 50% of what you spoke about. A week later and they most likely can't recall 10% of what you spoke about. Can you remember an in-depth conversation you had with someone on the phone two days ago?

❏ When calling someone back from a cold call, start out with your name, company name, and what you're calling about. Don't just start out with, *"This Is Joe. We spoke last week and you asked me to call you back."* That's soooooo stupid.

> **"Hello Jim. This is Jim Smith at National Systems. I spoke to you last week regarding the new copier, and you asked me to call you back today. Real briefly I just want to review what we spoke about."**

❏ If you know a person is sitting on the fence and you can't get them off, try this.

> **"Jake, I sense you're a little hesitant about going ahead with this. What are you concerned about that might happen? "**

Many times the prospect will tell you his real concern.

❏ When scheduling a call back try to set a specific date and time. Then ask them if they're usually in on that particular day. Many times a prospect will tell you to call back on a Wednesday not remembering he has his office meeting that day, or his golf day.

❏ Before hanging up on a call that's going to be a call back, quickly review what you spoke about.

> **"I'll be calling you Tuesday at 10. Your program will be on CD. We'll write the scripts and fax them to you, once you approve them, we'll then go into production and produce the program so you can hear it. There's no monthly or yearly fees and no contracts to get locked into, it's just**

a one-time investment of $500. Is that enough
information for you to be able to make a decision on this, or is there still something you're
not sure about?

If he's the decision maker and says he has enough information to make a decision, then just say,

"Since you know everything there is to know
about this, what's the absolute worst thing that
could happen if you went ahead with this today? "

This will weed out any hidden objections.

❑ Here's an interesting statement to make on a cold call.
If they seem interested and want a call back, ask them if they
consider themselves a good prospect. If they say yes or no,
ask them why. It's amazing what you'll hear.

❑ To find someone's interest level you can say,

"On a scale from 1-10, where would you say you
are?"

If they say 7, say,

"What would it take to get you to a 10? "

Often they'll tell you.

❑ Here's a good phrase to use when you want them to
do something for you.

"Is there any reason why ...?"

For example,

"Is there any reason why we can't get started
today?"

❑ If you've given your full presentation and you know
they have enough information to make a decision, but they
want you to call back, you can say,

*"I can do that, but what do you suggest we talk about
on our next call that you don't already know?* "

This gets them thinking why you need to call back. They

may just tell you to write up the order, or tell you don't bother to call back, if he's interested he'll call you. In that case you saved yourself a call back.

❑ Sometimes a person may ask you to call back in three months. You need to probe further because you may be able to call back sooner. If they tell you to call back because they're waiting on a new line of products, ask when they expect to get them. People just throw numbers out in a roundabout way. If they can't tell you when the changes will be taking place, move on.

❑ Many times a prospect will tell you they're going on vacation, a business trip, etc. and when they get back they'll buy from you. This is a good time to test how serious the person is. You can say things like,

X **"Great! What we can do then is get the paper-work started now, so when you get back everything will be ready to go."**

Or,

"Great, what I'll do is ask you some questions now, so that when you get back the order will be ready to ship."

With the On-Hold Message programs I sell, I say,

"When do you plan on getting back?"

Once they say a week or two, I tell them it will take us that long to write the scripts for them. I then just start writing up the order! If they're serious, they'll agree and think it's a good idea to get started now. If not, they're giving me an excuse.

❑ Don't beg for the business. If you've left three messages, voice mail, etc. and they don't return your calls, move on. They're telling you they decided not to buy. The more you pester them, the more desperate you seem. Use some of the techniques in this book to get them to return calls.

Here's a statistic that applies too just about all salespeople. At any given moment you probably have about 35% of your prospects that will never buy from you, or if they do, they'll chew you down so low on price, you'll feel bad you even made the sale. Be very critical of the prospects you want to pursue. Get rid of the non-buyers as soon as possible.

❏ Sometimes you have a customer who just won't get off the fence. To get an answer from them on the spot, say this.

"Jim, we've been talking about this for a month now. What's the real reason you're not going ahead with this?"

Or.

"What's the real reason why you'll never order this?"

I can assure you, you'll have an answer before you hang up. Keep in mind, if you've been chasing this person around, it's your fault. I've told you over and over, don't chase people around. There are three-hundred million people living in America and more than 12 million businesses. Are you telling me you can't find someone who really wants your offer?

❏ If people ask for references, say,

"I can do that. If the references check out, you're going to go ahead with this, right?"

As a joke I sometimes say,

"Do you want the good ones or the bad ones? "

Don't send references unless you can get a solid commitment from the person.

❏ For someone who tells you they want to shop around, you can say,

"What is it you're looking for in a _____ company?"

I say,

"What is it you're looking for in an On-Hold company?"

If they can't answer you, they're probably not that serious.

124

❏ If a customer tells you the info you sent them is sitting right on their desk, and they haven't had time to review it, say,

✗ **"Well as long as you have it right there, do you see the page that says ...?"**

Or,

"Can you just turn to page 15?"

This is an excellent opportunity to start reviewing it with them. That's a lot better than asking when you should call back.

❏ Ask people for their web site address. Let them know that you want to review it, so when you call them back, you'll have a better idea of their company. When you call back, a great way to start the conversation is to ask him something about it that would lead to the reason he should use your product. I say,

"I noticed while I was at your website you ship world wide. You must get a hundred or more calls a day. How do you keep from putting some of those people on-hold?"

It's a perfect opening for me to explain the benefits of my offer.

❏ In your notes, you should have a best time to call people back if you couldn't set a definite time and day to call back. I normally ask them if mornings or afternoons are usually a better time to reach them. The more specific the better. You could also find out from the receptionist.

❏ Sometimes a prospect will tell you he'll call you back later in the day or the next day. Give them your number and say,

"Mark, I know how busy it can get for you at a minutes notice. In case you don't have a chance to call me later/tomorrow, what would be a bet-

ter time/day for me to call you?"

If they're serious about the call back they'll tell you. If not, they'll say just try back whenever. Call backs are the false promises of future money. Get a no today, not next week.

❏ If you call someone back and they say they're still considering it, say: *What is it you're considering?* If they can't tell you, the only thing they're considering is how to get rid of you.

❏ Use a timer for call backs. If someone tells me to call back at 2:00 p.m., I set the timer for that time. This makes sure you'll never miss a call back. A lot of watches come with timers. Also, most contact management software programs have alarms built in.

❏ Here's a great little question to ask if they decide not to buy your product/service.

"Frank, are you saying that because you don't think you'll get a return back on your investment?"

Most of the time you'll find that's the reason.

❏ If you have someone who's not returning your calls, fax them this letter. My hit rate is a 75% response. I got this technique from Robert. L. Shook. This came from his book "I'll Get Back To You." It's filled with a bunch of unusual ways to get people to return your calls. Robert has some excellent books on phone sales and selling. Check them out.

A. B. C. Systems
"Security Specialists"

TO:_____DATE:_____
COMPANY:_____
FROM:_____

I'm sure there's a very good reason you haven't returned my calls. I don't want to be a nuisance, so just call or fax back your response and we'll take it from there.

_____ I'M OUT OF TOWN.

_____I'M BUSY ON MY DEADLINE. CALL ME NEXT WEEK.

_____CALL ME AT_____(TIME)ON_____(DATE)_____

_____I NO LONGER WORK HERE.

_____I PROMISE I'LL CALL YOU WITHIN THE NEXT WEEK.

_____IF IT WILL TAKE 10 MINUTES OR LESS, CALL ME NOW.

_____OTHER(FILL IN BELOW)

_____

_____

PHONE 1-800-0000   FAX 954-000-000
E-mail abcd@joe.net

127

20

Prospecting Tips

In this section I've compiled lots of tips on prospecting. These have made a lot of money for me, and will for you as well.

Prospect and Selling are Different

Never, never, never forget that *prospecting and selling are completely different things.* When you're prospecting, you're looking to find someone who's the decision maker, interested in your offer, and can afford it NOW! The selling begins after the person qualifies on those points. If they don't, you can throw all the greatest closing techniques at them you want, they simply won't do any good. Prospect first, sell second. Always remember that. I promise you, if you can learn to be a master prospector your sales will soar.

Qualify Quickly

Top phone reps qualify their prospects in about one minute. If they have no desire to speak with you, say goodbye. If they do want to speak with you, ask them qualifying questions. It's stupid to spend 15 minutes on the phone with someone who doesn't even qualify.

Prospect Everywhere

Don't just sell at work, *sell 24 hours a day.* Find prospects in the newspaper. Look for people who just got promoted. Check your local city business newspaper, since they usually list all the new companies opening, and some even have the owners' names and phone numbers. An excellent way to find companies that are expanding is to read the classifieds. If they're hiring people, that's good.

"Where Did You Get My Name?"

Here's a great ice breaker. Sometimes a prospect will ask you where you got their name. Without missing a beat, say

"Your name's on a list of people who are supposed to have a lot of money. Is that true?"

They'll burst out laughing. I've never had anyone do anything other than laugh.

Avoiding a Quick Brush Off

When you're speaking with someone who you think is the owner and he says he doesn't handle that type of purchase, and tries to pass you off to his secretary or office manager, that's a stall. Immediately respond with,

"I thought you were the owner?"

If he says yes, say,

"Since this will ultimately need to get your final approval, I'd like to first find out if this is something you'd be interested in. If you are, I'd be more than happy to talk with your office manger and send you a proposal. Can I ask you a couple of quick questions?"

I have found that 99% of the time the owner will ultimately sign off on the offer. If he sees a bill for $500 and doesn't have a clue how your product or service is a benefit to him, he'll cancel the order. Of course if you say "I thought you were the owner," and he says no, immediately respond with,

"What's the name of the owner?"

I don't know about you, but I've personally had my share of cancellations from people who push me off to someone else, only to see it fall through at the last minute. I refuse to talk to anyone else other than main decision makers unless he personally knows what I'm offering. If he doesn't want to listen, I move on.

It's Good When They're Busy

If a person says he's busy and the phone is ringing off the hook, say,

"That's the reason I'm calling."

No matter what you sell, if a company is very busy, they more than likely would make a good prospect for your product/service. When I call back, I say,

"Since you're so busy, how do you keep from putting people on-hold?"

Since I sell Telephone On-Hold Message programs, this is a good opening.You could also say,

"How do you keep your supplies in stock all the time? How do you keep up with all the paperwork? etc."

Point out a problem and give them the solution.

Get Alternative Numbers

If you call someone and they're not in, ask if there's another number they can be reached at. If they give you a cell phone number, ask the person if that's how they normally do business. If yes, call them.

Qualify!

Many salespeople fail because of poor qualifying. This shows a lack of respect for the customer and points out a lack of listening skills. Before launching into a full-blown presentation, ask questions right up front to make sure you're dealing with the decision maker, and if they actually qualify for your product or service. Trying to sell a $200,000 computer system to a two-man operation that makes $35,000 a year is plain stupid. Qualify, qualify, qualify!

Look for Unique Sources of Prospects

Ask yourself who your customers do business with. Here's an example. I sell Telephone On-Hold Message systems. I contact the vendors who *install* the phone systems. I tell them we produce on-hold messages and if a customer asks about them, would they call me. Many say yes! I send a package that explains our program and payment structure. Since I'm always looking for people who have phone systems, what better source is there than the people who install them? Some people will even give you their customer base to call. If you sell alarm systems, you may want to call on builders. Maybe you can pre-wire the homes, and when the people move in, they just need to call you. If you sell fences, call on swimming pool companies. Since pools need a fence around them, maybe you can be part of the package deal. Be creative and think, think, think!

Get the Name

If you don't know the name of the person you're calling, don't say, *"Who's in charge of the marketing for the company?"* Say,

"What's the name of the person who handles the marketing for the company?"

Most of the time they'll just tell you. Then just say,

"Is John in?"

If he is, you'll be surprised how often they put you through. If not, you'll know who to ask for the next time you call.

When to Hang Up

When you finish giving your presentation, always be the last one to hang up in case the customer has just one more question. When you're prospecting, you hang up first if the customer's not interested.

Ask for Other Departments to Get In

If you just can't get through to the person you want to talk to, call back and ask to speak to someone in the sales department, customer service dept., etc. When the person picks up, say,

"They were transferring me to Bob Smith. Can you put me through to him please?"

Most of the time they will.

Tell Them Who You Are Holding For

If you call a company and the operator picks up and says, *"ABC Corp., please hold,"* without missing a beat say,

"Holding for John Smith please."

Many times the operator's so busy, she'll just put you through without asking what the call's about. It's also good time management. You won't have to stay on hold every time.

Four Rings is Enough

When calling someone, let the phone ring four times only. After that, they're too busy to talk. This is also good time management.

Get the Name of the Replacement

If the screener says so-and-so no longer works here, without missing a beat say,

"What's the name of the person who took his place?"

Don't ask "Who" took his place. That just sets them up to start asking what the call's about.

How to Address Them

Back to names ... if a person's name on your lead sheet says Michael, call him Michael unless he comes to the phone and says, "Mike speaking." Then you should call him Mike. Don't shorten the name unless they do.

Call Every Name on the List

Don't skip around your lead list trying to pick names of people you think would be a prospect. There's no way you can know that. Just dial straight through your list.

Work the List Backwards

When calling from an association list, always start from the letter Z and work forward. Everyone else starts at A, and never gets to the people in the back of the book. Those people very seldom get called.

Find the Influencer

Keep in mind that there's always the main decision maker, and sometimes the *influential* decision maker. That person can be a manager, comptroller, spouse, etc. When they tell you they want to run it by someone like that, try to talk with the other person. More than likely if they shoot it down, the main decision maker will follow along.

A Great Reference Directory for Prospects

A good way for you to find out about associations: Go to the library and ask for the *"Encyclopedia of Associations."* There are several volumes. They'll tell you how to order various association books and directories, how much, etc. You normally can't check these books out. They're used for reference purposes so bring a pad and pen.

Use Small Talk if they Initiate It

If by chance, when talking with a prospect who brings up a subject that's not related to business, and you know something about it, don't be afraid to tell him. Since I live in Florida, a lot of my prospects and customers tell me they went to Disney World years ago. I normally tell them how things have changed and usually throw in a short humorous story. ONLY DO THIS IF THEY INITIATE IT! Otherwise, just stick to business. You're not calling for a conversation. You're calling to ask for their business.

If Delegated Down, Learn the Position

If the decision maker is interested in what you have to offer, he may delegate it to someone else. Always ask him what that person's position is. If he tells you to talk with his receptionist, this is not a good sign. Working with the VP or head of marketing, purchasing, etc., is a lot better.

"Hi"

Instead of starting your opening statement with good morning or good afternoon. Start it with *"Hi."* It's shorter, saves time, and sounds friendly.

"Hi Jim, this is Susan Smith with ..."

Ask About Their Decision-Making Process

If you call on someone for the first time, and they say they looked into getting your product/service but decided it wasn't for them, ask them what led them to that decision. Many times people tell me they were quoted a thousand dollars for a Telephone On-Hold system. When I tell them we have no monthly or yearly fees, and no contracts to get locked into, and it's a one-time investment of just $500, they are more inclined to listen.

Ask What Time They'll Get the Message

When leaving a message for someone with the receptionist, always ask them what time the person will be getting the message. If they say around two, you can call back then.

Learn the Pronunciation

Make sure you know how to pronounce the person's name. When you stumble around attempting to say it, the screener perceives you as a telemarketer. If you're not sure, just ask for the person by their first name.

Giving Too Much Info Can be Detrimental

On a cold call, if the person you're trying to contact is not in, don't leave your name and number with the receptionist when she asks you for it. Just say,

> **"That's ok, I'll just try back, thank you."**
> *(click)*

I never leave my name, company name, or any other info if the prospect's not in. If the receptionist knows you're the same person calling back, you'll annoy them and they'll never put you through.

Fax the Tough-to-Reach Prospects

If you have trouble getting to the decision maker, just send him a fax. If you sent five faxes a day, five days a week, that would be 100 extra prospects a month you'd be directly contacting. I normally send faxes when I'm down to those last few names in my leads that are never in. Fax before 9:00 a.m. or after 5:00 p.m. The key is to put the person's name at the top of it so they'll get it. If there's no name on it, most people will throw it away thinking it's a fax broadcast (which it really is). By putting their name on it, it's more personalized and will be read by just about everyone you send it to. Let them know you've been trying to reach them because there's a good possibility you may be able to do business together. Use the "killer" voice mail script for your letter. You can also try to email them.

How to REALLY Build Rapport

If your prospect has you on a speaker phone, and tells you to hold a moment because he wants someone else to hear what you have to offer, you may have a two-to-three minute wait until the other person gets to the office. To fill that time, some reps ask dumb questions like how's the weather, have you lived there all your life, etc. Instead of the garbage chit-chat that you think will bond you with your prospect, use that time to learn more about the person. Ask him how he got into his type of industry. He'll open right up and tell you quite a bit about himself. He'll be doing 90% of the talking while you just give him praise for his achievements. That's how to really build rapport with a prospect.

Qualify!

Don't waste time blabbing to unqualified people. If in the first minute you find the person you're talking to is not a prospect or not qualified, immediately end the call. No asking about the weather, no telling them you visited their town, you have relatives who live there, etc. They don't care and you're wasting time. Get on to your next call.

Stand Up and Sell

Throughout the day, consider giving your presentation while you're standing up. It gives you a good boost of energy that reflects back to your prospect. If you're working full time on the phones and you're not standing up pitching every so often, I can assure you, by the end of the day you'll be sounding flat.

Be Sure Your Leads are Fresh

If you have to purchase your own lead lists, only order what you or your company can dial in thirty days. Business list companies have told me that lists go bad at a rate of 1%

per week. Sales lists will normally have about 10% disconnects or wrong numbers. If you're getting more than that, find another list broker.

Call Earlier for Best Results

The American Teleservices Association says you're *five times* as likely to reach your prospect on the first attempt calling between nine and ten in the morning. Adjust your leads according to time zone. This one statistic alone can increase your contact rate five-fold! Would that work for you?

Is Long Distance a Benefit?

Don't tell people you're calling from out of state right up front. Some people will automatically rule you out because of that. I tell them after building rapport with them. If I'm calling someone in my own state, I'll tell them what city I'm calling from. Some people feel that by telling the receptionist you're calling long distance it is an advantage, and you'll be put through to the decision maker more often. I feel you should use what works best for the industry you're calling.

Be an Expert Qualifier

Invest more time with *serious* prospects, and minimize the time spent chasing "shoppers." Just because they spoke to you once doesn't necessarily make them good. Become an expert on qualifying prospects. Rate them on a scale from 1-10. If they rate lower than eight, don't spend too much time chasing them. Top producers know who to keep working and who to get rid of and replace with a new prospect. You want quality prospects. You know you're reading people well when your 8-10's are buying 75% of the time. If they're not, this method will teach you how to qualify them better.

Cut the Slang, Buddy

Never speak to people using slang, it makes you come off as uneducated. Cool man, I'm your home boy, awesome, etc.

Set a New Prospect Goal

Depending on your industry, you should set a daily goal of how many new prospects you want to find each day. I personally try to find five qualified prospects each day. If you can do that on a regular basis, your sales will soar. In my industry, a good phone rep can close 20-25% of those prospects. It's a lot easier to have the mindset that you're going to find five prospects rather than you have to make a hundred calls today.

Have a Plan, and Stick to It

Don't call someone up to have a conversation about nothing. Make sure the person knows that you're calling for their business and nothing else.

When They ask About Company Size ...

If a customer asks if your company is large or small, use that to your advantage.

If it is small, tell them,

> **"The owner likes to keep it small, so we can give more personalized service, and keep the overhead low so we can pass those savings onto you."**

If it's large, tell them,

> **"Because of the size of the orders we put into our vendors, you get a substantial discount that we pass on to you."**

As you can see, you can use the small or large company image to your favor. Large or small, make sure they understand they're dealing with a major organization, not just an individual.

If They Hang Up on You, Move On

If someone hangs up on you, don't waste your time calling back and asking them why. That's a waste of time and shows your desperation. Ask yourself, Do you really want to argue and fight with people and try to prove you are right, or do you want to make sales? Just dial the next number on your list and move on.

Consider the Source

Always consider the source of your information.Getting info about the company from the VP is a lot better than getting it from the receptionist. (However, some receptionists DO know more about the company than some VP's & owners!)

Consider a Weekend Call

Depending on the type of person or industry your calling, many people can be called on Saturdays. If you have a hard-to-reach prospect, you may want to try on a Saturday morning.

Words That Really Mean "NO"

Over the years I've found certain words and phrases that appear to be positive, but when you read between the lines, they almost always mean "no." Here are some.

- *"I'm going to think about this seriously."*

Ask him what he plans on thinking about. He won't be able to tell you.

- *Complimenting you on your selling skills or telling you you're a good salesperson, or saying, "You can work for me anytime."*

Ask him if he's so impressed with your skills why he's not going to do business with you.

- *"I'm going to consider this next year."*

Call his bluff: **"I'll mark you on my calender for next February 19th at 10 AM, is that good for you?"**

- *"I want to do it but not at this time."*

Yeah, maybe in his next life.

- *"We haven't had time to make a decision yet."*

I've replied with, **"How much time do you need, forever?"** If the person laughs nervously, he's scared to death he'll have to make a decision.

- *Refuses to schedule the next step in your sales process.*

If he was serious, wouldn't it be logical to want to go to the next step?

- *When a prospect uses the word **interesting,** this usually means no.*

Ask her what's so interesting about it? If she starts telling you benefits, tell her since she sees the benefits this could have for her, why she's not going to order it? Some of you may not agree with everything I said, so I suggest you try the responses out for yourself.

Follow Your System

To be the tops in your field, you have to have a method and system. You have to know why you're doing certain things. Nothing you do should ever be haphazard. You need to know every detail of the system you've incorporated to be successful. There are no gray areas in selling. Everything is black and white.

Start at the Top

Depending on the price of your product or service, the final decision maker may not always be the owner, president or CEO of the company. But, you should always start high. You're more likely to get referred down than up. If you're selling a high ticket item, you have to get to the top person. They're the one who's going to be writing the check. If you're selling a $50 magazine subscription, the office manager can handle that. Since you're not talking about a large amount of money, many managers could just take it out of petty cash. The more expensive your product or service, the higher up the corporate ladder it will have to go to get approval. If you sell an item for $100 or less, and have been going through a hard time reaching the owner, you can step down a notch and go to the office manager. Many don't need authority for a small purchase, but always start at the top.

Move Forward

Try to take each call as far as you can. This doesn't mean trying to cram your pitch down their throat as soon as they pick up the phone. What it means is that when the person asks you a question, after answering it, you respond with another question to keep the conversation going.

If Your Name is Unusual ...

If you have an unusual last name, it can work for, or against you. If it's something like Wojokiecowitz, I would suggest you use a different last name or shorten it. I suggest something like Jones, Johnson, Powers, Miller, Andrews, etc. Also, there's no need to tell people what nationality you are. I've heard reps say things like, "It's pronounced Pole-an-skee. It's a Polish name." Some people are prejudiced and may not like your nationality type.

Call a Lawyer

Perhaps you sometimes hear, "I need to run it by my lawyer." Yeah, right. Unless you're selling a product or service that does need an attorney to review contracts, then fine. If not, call their bluff:

"I understand. What's his number? I'll need to speak with him personally just to make sure he fully understands what we'll be doing for you and how I should proceed."

In my entire selling career, I've never spoken to a single attorney. Never! Not one single person gave me their number. If he gives you the number, great. If not, thank you and good-bye.

Put Your Business Card to Work

There are two types of business cards: stationary and interactive. Stationary is when it just mentions your name, and what you do. For example, Jim Smith, ABC Realtors. Interactive is when it asks the person to start the sales process. Here's an example. The back of my business card reads: "Free moneymaking sales tips! Go to www..." It asks them to act. If you're a Realtor, you could put on the back of your card, "To view listings of our homes, go to our web site at www.homesforsale.com." If you sell a product, you can say, "Present this card and receive a 10% discount." If you offer a service, you could offer one free week. A chiropractor could offer a free consultation. Use your card to motivate people to act. Make your business card an interactive sales tool.

Leave Business Cards Everywhere

Here's an unusual idea that you may want to try. Some people put their business card in all their bills they mail out. The reasoning is that a *person* has to open the envelope to get the bill out. In doing so, they'll automatically see your card and read it. I learned this from a person selling real estate.

Since he sold locally, he did this with his bills that were going to local companies. He actually got business from this! Your business cards aren't doing you any good hidden away in your wallet or purse. Leave them in restrooms, on restaurant tables, on cars, etc. GET YOUR NAME OUT AND LET PEOPLE KNOW WHAT YOU SELL!

E-Mail Them if They Won't Call Back

Often you'll talk to someone who seems interested in your offer, but when you call back, they're never in or won't come to the phone. I always make it a point to ask people for their web site or e-mail address. If they're not returning your calls, e-mail them. If they don't respond to that, you don't have a buyer.

The "Present Supplier" Stall

If someone tells you they've been using the same supplier for years, just say,

> **"Since you've been with them so long, how do you know you're still getting the best price, product, service?"**

Regardless of the reply, say,

> **"Jim, since I have you on the phone, let me give you some of our prices/rates so you can at least make a comparison. Do you ..."**

And just start into your presentation. Many times they'll want to hear your prices.

Should You Leave a Message or Not?

I don't agree or disagree with this next technique, so you'll have to judge it for yourself.

When you call a business and the receptionist tells you the person is not in, and asks if you would like to leave a message, you have two choices.

1. You can say, "No thanks, I'll try back." Click.

2. You can say, "Tell him Joe Catal called, and I'll try him back tomorrow."

The reasoning behind the second response is to get your name in front of as many people as possible. When you do call

called twice. They'll think it must be important if you're calling back. I've used the second technique and can tell you it
works. Sometimes they'll ask why I didn't leave a message
with the receptionist. I say

> **"The reason I wanted to speak with you per-
> sonally is ... "**

And then I go into my presentation. As usual, try it, if you
like the results, great, if not, drop it. But do keep in mind, by
leaving your name with someone every time you make a call,
you're taking time away from your dialing.

How to Respond to a Negative Comment

If a prospect says something negative about your product or service, say,

> *"Are you saying that because of what somebody told
> you about it?"*

This is an excellent question. It works on several levels.
First, many people hear things from other people that may not
be true. Just because someone had a bad experience with
your product or service, doesn't mean it's not for anyone else.
Maybe that person bought the cheapest model that fell apart
in six months. Maybe your service didn't fit their particular
situation. They may also tell you they read articles on your
product/service. Maybe they just personally don't like it. This
question will get them to explain.

A Simple, But Effective, Lead Source

Earlier in the book I mentioned how to use association
directories to find prospects. Besides calling on your existing
accounts, here's another idea you may not have considered,
but you probably already pay for it. The newspaper. See who's
advertising. Look in the business section and see who just
got a promotion. Who's taking over a new company? See who
just had a new baby. With the new addition, does that mean
they have to increase their insurance? Look for people who
just got married or bought a new home. Send them a con-
gratulation note with your card. Look for people who just made
a real estate transaction. Look through the classifieds for companies hiring, that's always a good sign. Look in the classifieds

for people selling expensive cars or boats. Often these are people with unlisted numbers! That's a goldmine. Buy the auto trader and boat trader magazines, they'll have tons of people to call. Many cities have a business newspaper that lists names and numbers of businesses that just opened.

When You're Put on Hold

If you're talking with someone who puts you on hold, when they come back on say, *"As I was saying...,"*and just continue where you left off.

Write Down Their Name

If someone calls you, always write their name down immediately. You don't want to have to ask them what their name is again. Also write down any other name they give you.

Listen to Their On-Hold Message

If you're placed on hold when you call a company, pay attention. If they have an on-hold message program, you can learn some things about them. **"I noticed when I was on-hold your message said you can ship worldwide. Do you do a lot of business overseas?"**

Research Their Website

Get names and leads from websites. Many times the site will list the owner's name. They'll also list their phone number and address. When the person you want to talk to comes to the phone, start out with,

"I was looking through your web site and ..."

Questions You Need to Answer in Your Opening

During the first 30 seconds of your call, people want to know,

Who you are,

why are you calling, and,

what's in it for them.

Make sure those elements are in your opening statement.

Pay for Their Gas

If someone has to drive a long distance to see you, offer to pay for their gas.

An E-Mail Prospecting Format

Whenever sending an e-mail to a company you want to do business with, use this format.

State who you are, what you do, what you want, and the best way to proceed.

Here's an example of mine.

> **Hi. My name's Joe Catal. I work for ABC Corp. We specialize in producing Telephone On-Hold Message programs for collision shops.**
>
> **I'd like to send one of our information packages to the owner, manager, or person who handles this type of decision for the company.**
>
> **Can you please tell me the best way to proceed? Thank you.**

Instead of trying to sell them, try and get to the decision maker for an appointment to talk. You'll find that at least 20-30% of the people will respond to you. Some will say they're not interested, and others will tell you who to contact. Also, if you don't know the name of the person you should contact, in the subject box of your e-mail write, "Doing business with your company." You're almost guaranteed they'll read it. If you know the persons name, use that. Don't send your message as an attachment, do a copy and paste. I personally don't open attachments from anyone I don't know. People are afraid of viruses. Notice how it's spaced? That's so it's easier to read. This is really a killer way to get business. It's not spamming, because you're making a legitimate inquiry on how you should proceed. Don't send more than 20 out at a time. If your Internet provider sees hundreds of e-mails coming from you, they'll want to know why.

Sell More in the Same Area

If you sell nationally, once you make a sale in a particular city, you can go to the Internet and look up similar companies in their city from the yellow page directories. You'll just need to type in the zip code and it will bring up all the companies you're looking for in that particular region. Be aware, some people may not want to be used as a reference, so ask them first.

Call From Corporate Headquarters

To give your cold calls more credibility in the eyes of the screener, you can say,

"This is Joe Catal calling from ABC Corporate Headquarters."

Saying *corporate headquarters* sounds very important. If you've done business overseas, you can even say world headquarters.

Ways to Address Them

Always use your first and last name when introducing yourself to a prospect for the first time. It sounds more professional than just "Bob's calling."

As for asking the receptionist for the person by name, you can ask by their first name, or first and last. I usually ask by first name.

I also speak to the customer by their first name: **"Hello Bob, this is Joe Catal."**

Saying Mr. or Mrs. is all right. If they answer the phone by starting out with Mr. or Mrs., say their name that way. **"Hello Mr. Smith, this is Joe Catal."**

Never say "sir." This puts you in a lower position than them.

With doctors I usually say Dr. Smith. For clergy I usually say Rabbi, Father etc. Whenever calling on homeowners, always say Mr., Ms., or Mrs.

Ask Them Why

Sometimes you'll call a prospect who'll say, "It's funny you called, we were just thinking about something like this," or, "We were just discussing this last week."

Your immediate response should be,

"Why are you considering something like this?"

Or,

"Why are you considering a service like this? "

They'll tell you everything you need to know to close the sale. *Why are you considering* is a very powerful phrase. It's a killer question to ask on and inbound call.

If They Are At Another Number ...

Sometimes when you call a business, the person will tell you that Frank Dooblevitz is at another number. Say,

"What's that number please?"

After they give you the number say,

"What extension is that?"

You'll be surprised how many times you'll get the direct extension. This means you can avoid the screener. If by chance a secretary does answer, just say,

"Extension 100 please."

Usually she'll just put you through. If she asks what it's about, say,

"I called your other location and was told I should talk to Jim directly. Would you tell him I'm on the line please? "

Niche Selling

Most salespeople, even the best ones, have better success rates selling to certain individuals or industries. Perhaps it's a mental comfort zone, or a fit with their personality type. Whatever the reason, if you see this trend, stick with them! If you're a manager or business owner and you know certain employees make more sales selling to a particular group, try to get that person more of those type of leads. Use your strenghts, or your employees' to their fullest.

Talk to a Person

Always remember to talk *to* the person, *not at*. Many reps just read their scripts without realizing there's a person on the other end of the phone. Don't just be a robot, memorize your opening statement and script. Add some personality.

Selling Yourself

Here's a great opening statement to use if you're looking for a job. Call the company and say to the person in charge of setting up the interview,

> "Hi, this is Debbie Smith. I'm calling regarding the sales position. I've been very successful in phone sales and I'd just like to ask you a few questions to see if it's worthwhile for us to schedule an appointment. Do you have a moment to talk?"

This will definitely separate you from the people who just call up and say they're calling about the sales job.

"Mommy's in the Bathroom Right Now."

If you work out of your home, make sure kids never answer the phone. You should have a separate business line that no one picks up but yourself. Also, no barking dogs, screaming kids and loud music in the background. This is just really stupid, yet it happens every day.

Empty Your Mouth

Never eat or chew gum while talking with customers. I'm amazed when I walk into phone rooms and see people eating lunch and talking to customers at the same time.

Paging Might Not Be the Best Option

If a receptionist says she'll page the person you're calling, ask her if that's the way they normally take their calls. If not, you may be interrupting them from a meeting.

Find Out if There are Other Decision Makers

After you qualify someone, and they tell you they're the decision maker, say,

> "It's nice to work with someone who can make a decision on their own, without having to go to a committee."

If they're not the decision maker, to save face they'll tell you they want to run it by their crew, manager, etc. That tells you there's more than one decision maker.

What Do You REALLY Sell?

What do you really sell? What I really sell is how business owners can increase their annual sales 2%-4% year-in and

and year-out from a single one-time investment of just $400. If you're an accountant, you could say you show business owners how they can keep more of what they make without having to pay it to the IRS. What do you sell? People aren't interested in the product or service you sell, just what it can do for them. You buy a drill because of the hole it makes, not because it's a drill.

21

Selling Large Corporate Accounts

If you're selling to a large company, you'll more than likely have to talk with many different people. Each individual needs to be sold a different way depending on his position in the company. Here are the four buyer types.

1. Economic buyer.

2. User buyer.

3. Technical buyer.

4. The coach.

I learned this concept from Stephen E. Heiman's book *"New Strategic Selling." (ISBN: 0446673463)*

This book is for people who sell to large companies, and have several different people to talk to, or work with. It's an excellent read, and will open you up to new ideas and concepts. The most important being you can't give your same presentation to each of the different people involved. You really need to talk to each a different way. Here are some concepts I use.

Each one of these people will look at your offer from a different point of view. One person may have more than one buyer role. The **economic buyer** is the person who gives FINAL approval to buy your product or service. He's looking to make sure his investment will get a return on his money, improve efficiency, etc. He has to be shown that your product or service is an improvement over what they're currently using. Sell this person on benefits, not technical jargon.

The **user buyer** person is the one who will actually use your product/service. This could be one person or a group. This group is generally comprised of the employees of the company. Since most people do not like change, they're more concerned with how much they'll have to learn. If they don't learn how to use it, will they be fired? Will this actually save them time? Make them more productive? Talk to these people about ease of learning, how other people similar to them have had great success with your product, you being there if they have any questions, how they'll be more productive, how you can make their life easier, etc.

A perfect example is of a company getting their first computer. They'll feel uncomfortable and not sure if they can learn it. Let these people know you'll hold their hand throughout the whole setup.

The *technical buyer* is the person who has a lot of influence on the final decision maker. This is the person who is responsible for all the technical aspects. With new computers, for example, they'll be the one putting in the new programs, fixing it when it crashes, changing ink cartridges on printers, etc. If they feel it's too much work or it will have them working an extra 10 hours a week to keep it up and running, they'll shoot it down. You really need to work with this person! If they're not sure about something, explain it in detail. The final decision maker will ALWAYS check with the technical person to make sure the technical person feels comfortable that he can implement the program.

The *coach* is key throughout the entire process. This is the person who's usually in middle management. They may or may not have a lot of power in the company, but they know the names of the people you should be talking to. They'll help you get your foot in the door. Many times we make calls to people who seem to want to help us. Maybe they really like what we have to offer and since they can't make the decision on their own, they'll forward your info or even let you talk directly to the person who can make the purchase. He's kind of like having a friend who works for the company.

You can call him on a regular basis throughout the sales process and ask things like,

> **"How long does it usually take to get an approval on something like this?"**
>
> **"What type of person is John like?"**

The coach will be happy to help you out. Keep in mind,

the coach is helping you because he himself likes what you have to offer. I always say to a coach,

"Jim, if it were your decision alone, would you buy it?"

Also ask the coach what he likes about your offer. What benefits could he see? A coach is different than having a receptionist say you can reach Jim at 1-800... She's just doing her job. A coach genuinely wants to help you. Understanding your buyer's role will put you light years ahead of other sales reps.

This structure I've just outlined is normally used where there are multiple decision makers such as large companies, government entities, school districts, or franchises. On smaller companies with only one owner, she'll be playing all four roles alone. Understanding the concepts in this book will definitely boost your sales. I use it all the time. It's an excellent weapon to add to your arsenal.

Other Large Account Tips

Here are more brief tips on working with larger accounts.

Nurture Your Big Accounts

If you've been selling for a while, you probably have a few big accounts. Be very protective of those accounts! Think of ways to increase your business with them. If you have large accounts you're doing little or no business with, ask yourself why is that? What can you think of to position yourself better? Try to find people in their company who can help you do more business with them.

Pay special attention to accounts that may be small now, but will be growing in the future. Many people miss this opportunity. The huge corporations and franchises have vendors who grew with them. How do you think they got those accounts? Be aware of phrases such as: we're expanding, or, we're opening additional locations. Find out how you can get the business for those other locations.

Sell to a Group

Selling to a group is a lot easier then selling to an individual. Giving your presentation to a group of people who are listening on a speaker phone is to your advantage. You can answer everyone's questions, and if the group is being positive, the rest will follow. Also, if the people in the group are giving you their names, be sure to write them down. If for some reason you have trouble reaching the decision maker again, you'll have a name of someone else you can talk too.

Address Everyone on the Conference Call

When speaking to a group of people over a speakerphone, address questions to everyone, not one specific person. After describing a feature you would say,

"Does anyone have any questions about that? Is everyone clear on that point?"

Here's a killer closing question to ask a group after you've answered all of their questions,

"Is there anyone who thinks this wouldn't be a benefit to the company?"

What a killer! Everyone will look at each other because nobody wants to take the blame for a bad decision. If it makes sense to the group, they'll all just follow along.

When You Stumble Upon a Huge Prospect...

Sometimes we get those rare occasions to call on a customer who's a big gun in the industry. Maybe they have 50 locations, the largest company, etc. You had no clue who this company was. You were just minding your own business dialing down your list, and boom! You somehow got to the decision maker and he starts asking you questions that involve a lot of money. Maybe your average order is $500, and he's looking at ten to twenty thousand dollars of business. At the end of this book, I'll recommend books that specifically deal with this type of selling. For now, here's what I like to do. First and foremost, understand that top CEO's generally like to talk to other CEO's. They'll more than likely delegate you to someone else. This is OK, as long as they heard your presentation and want to pursue it further. Once you have submitted your proposal, have the owner of your company call the CEO personally. Make sure when they call they tell the receptionist that it's the owner or president of the company. 99% of the time, a CEO always talks to an owner or president of a company. Here's what the owner of your company should say,

> **"I'm simply calling to introduce myself. As you know, we're trying to get your business for the _____. As the owner/president of ABC Corp., we regard your business as significant. If we are fortunate enough to get it, I'll personally see to it that you get the highest quality service and product on the market. Do you have any questions I can answer for you about our offer?"**

This is an excellent opening statement. If the customer has no questions, just thank him for taking the time to speak with you, and that you look forward to a long term relationship with his company. If he does have a question, make sure you know what the deal is about.

Another Conference Call Tip

If you're talking with two or more people on a speaker phone, and they say they want to talk it over, say,

"Great, I'll hold while you discuss it."

They may tell you they need more time and tell you to call back. They may also just say ok and put you on hold. It doesn't hurt to ask.

22

Customer Service

Keep this in mind, if you make the buying experience a pleasant one for your customer, you increase your odds dramatically on selling them again. That's long term thinking.

Answer on the Third Ring

You should answer your phone on or during the third ring. If you pick up on the first ring, you might sound rushed and sound like the person calling you is a nuisance. By the second ring you can stop what you're doing and prepare for the call. On the third ring you're ready for the call.

Designate a "Customer Service Calling Day"

If you've been in sales a while, you may have hundreds of accounts. If you spend just 20% of your time calling back people who already bought from you, along with prospecting for new business, you'd increase your sales dramatically. I personally use Fridays to call on existing customers. If you're a manager, consider making Friday customer service day. Everyone in the company calls existing customers only. Your sales will soar and you'll also save on leads. I've personally never come across a method as powerful as this. As a general rule, everyone knows Friday's aren't the best day of the week to cold call. You'll have a much better chance of making a sale to an existing customer on a Friday, than on a cold call. Also, not all salespeople like to service their accounts. This will ensure everyone is servicing them. Try it for one month, I guarantee you'll never go back to cold calling on Fridays. If you don't have a lot of accounts, I've found cold calling on Friday between 3:00 pm and 5:00 pm to be quite productive.

Return Calls Promptly

Always return calls to your customers promptly, good or bad. If I have a problem with someone, I take care of it first thing in the morning. I don't want to be thinking about it all day. If a customer calls you once, it's a problem. If he has to call you again, it's a complaint. Remember, once you solve a problem for someone and they're happy, it's a great time to ask for a referral! Always be thinking of how you can turn a negative into a positive.

No Whining!

Make sure you never complain or whine to a customer! I hear it all the time...people telling me the service department's a mess...they really need to make changes around here... I'm not feeling good today...my kid's home sick, etc. No matter what, you're always doing fine and business is booming! If you're a business owner, make sure employees don't whine to customers. It's bad for the image of the company.

Add Value With Websites

For added value, give your customers a list of websites to go to about sales and marketing. They can see new ideas and concepts on how to generate more sales.

> **"John, I was on the Internet last night, and I went to a site I thought you'd like to go to, you have a pen?"**

Once they write it down, I ask them if they're interested in updating their program, or want to put an order in. What type of websites would your customers like to look at? You can use this as a good reason to call back when you want them to reorder.

Project a 24/7 Image

Never tell a customer you go home at five. If for some reason you can't call a person back at a certain time, always tell them you have an outside appointment. As far as my custumers are concerned, I don't eat, sleep, or drink. I'm there for them 24 hours a day. That's a great image to project. Also, there's no law that states you can't call someone from your home. So what if it costs you $2 for the call. Isn't it worth it to you to make the sale? I do this a lot for my West coast prospects.

An Ending to Avoid

Don't end your call with: have a nice day. That's so stale. I say,

> **"Jim, I know your busy and have to get back to work, I'll talk to you tomorrow. Now go make some money."**
>
> Or, **"... have a profitable day."**

How can you end your call that's a little different?

What Type of Selling Do You Do?

I believe there are three types of selling situations: Win/ win, win/lose, lose/ win. Win/win is when both you and your customer had a winning sales transaction. Win/lose is when you win and the customer loses. Maybe you gave him a higher price than normal, or a bad deal all around. Lose/win is when the prospect chews you so far down in price that it's not even worth it to do the deal, but you do it anyway just to make a sale. All transactions should be win/win. If they're not, some- one gets hurt and it's normally you.

Things to Remember About Customers

Keep in mind, your customers are someone elses pros- pects. Treat them so well that they'd feel guilty even consid- ering another competitor. Great customer service kills your competition.

And once you get a new customer, always keep this in mind. Never forget a customer. Never let a customer forget you. Keep them reminded that you're their official vendor.

Don't Cough at Them

This should seem obvious, but never clear your throat or cough into the phone. It really grosses out the person on the other end, and you come across as a real low-life. If you must, cover the phone with your hand so they can't hear you. Or hit the mute button if you have one.

Call Right Back if Disconnected

If you're talking with a prospect and accidentally get dis- connected, call right back. Just let them know you don't know how it happened. I usually make a joke of it and say,

"That's how we start a relationship with our customers, we hang up on them!"

This usually evokes a laugh and you can continue where you left off.

Call After the Sale

After a sale, always call your customer back and make sure they're happy with everything. It's also a great time to ask for a referral. This really makes you stand out from the crowd. Always let your customer know you'll be following up to make sure they're 100% happy.

They Don't Care About Your Policy

Never use the phrase, *"It's our company policy."* People don't want to hear about rules and policies. They want to hear how you can help them with their problem. Tell them what you can do, not what you can't.

Understand the Reorder Cycle for Your Products

Depending on what you are selling, there's an average cycle of when people will order it again. It could be weekly, monthly, yearly, etc. Knowing these cycles is very important and overlooked by salespeople. With the on-hold messages I sell, I know that most people update their programs every 12-18 months. Sure I call them throughout the year, but I know that my best chance to resell them is during that 12-18 month period. What's the buying cycle for your product or service?

Surprise them With Something Extra

Make them feel like you gave them something special. Do you normally throw a little something extra into a deal as a free giveaway? Don't tell them about it at the beginning of your calls, tell them about it when you ship the product. If you sell copiers and automatically give people a free case of copier paper when they make a purchase, save that information and use it as something special your throwing in for the customer. For example,

"Jim, to show our appreciation for your business, we're throwing in a free case of copier

paper to get you started."

The customer will feel as if he's getting something special, even though they would have gotten the paper anyway.

Consolidate and Increase Orders

Here's a good idea on how to get larger orders and help your customers out. If you work in an industry that has people ordering from you on a weekly or biweekly basis, such as office supplies, cleaning supplies, copier paper, etc., look through your accounts and find people who order the same type of products over and over on a weekly or biweekly basis. For example, Susan Jones at ABC Corp. orders five cases of copier paper every week. Since most companies give discounts for volume orders, do this. Call Susan and tell her she's paying $400 a month on her copier paper by ordering five cases on a weekly basis. Tell her if she ordered all 20 cases at once, she could save 10% or $40 a month. That's almost $500 a year in savings! This does several things. It's a lot easier on your company to make only one trip to her business instead of four. The second is you're helping her save money. This is just good business practice. The third is, your orders will be larger. Wouldn't you rather get a commission on a $400 deal instead of $100?

Before Ending the Order Call...

Here's an excellent statement to say to someone after you've written the order and are ready to hang up.

> **"Susan, I want to thank you very much for your business. We don't take it lightly, and if there's anything we can do to improve our service to you, please call me personally and let me know, OK?"**

This is really a nice way to end a call.

Take Responsibility for Errors

Many people/companies do not want to take responsibility for their own mistakes. If you make one, tell the customer it was your fault and apologize. Don't try to talk your way out of it or blame someone else. If someone ordered ten cases and you shipped eight, immediately tell them it was your fault.

Apologize and take care of it NOW! Ship it overnight if you have to. People don't mind so much if a mistake was made. What shows your customer the type of company you are, is how quickly you respond to problems. Never forget that! When was the last time someone at a company told you they were wrong? By admitting the error, it shows you're a high level company. This is how top reps keep accounts for years. If you work for a company that has poor customer service, slip this under your boss's door for him to read. Poor customer service shows lack of respect for the customer, salespeople and the company in general. If you're working for someone like that, move to another company.

Don't "Try." DO It!

Substitute the word *"try,"* with **"will."** Don't tell someone you'll try to have the info to them by the end of the day. Tell them you **will** have it to them by the end of the day. "Try" is a negative word. By using *"will"* you're taking responsibility for an action that will be taken by you! People with poor time management or who aren't organized generally use "try" because using "will" would put them in a responsibility mode. This type of person doesn't want to be held accountable for anything. Listen to how superstars talk. You'll never hear them say "try." I truly believe that word is one of the worst words a salesperson, or any person in a company can use. Make that word illegal to say in your office. There's nothing better to a customer than to hear the person on the other end say,

"Mike, I will personally make sure you have it by Wednesday, OK?"

People who can't make commitments to customers or their employees are dragging everyone down. They're the losers of the company. From now on, take "try" out of your vocabulary.

Get Positive Word-of-Mouth

My experience is that a person will pay 10 percent more for a product or service if the customer service is good. And it's widely quoted that people who get top notch customer service will tell an average of 9-12 other people. If you're not getting referrals, you're not giving good customer service. Why wouldn't someone recommend people to you if they're happy with your product/service? When people receive poor service they tell up to 20 people! No matter what business you're in, there are some people you'll never please, just keep it to a minimum, or get rid of the customer for the good of the company.

Be Customer-Friendly

Have a customer-friendly attitude. Here are words all businesses should have on each employee's office wall. *Friendly, responsive, courteous, efficient, pleasant, helpful, caring, prompt.* That pretty much says it all.

Call Past Customers

If you call on a customer who hasn't purchased from you in awhile, open the call like this: after identifying yourself and telling them you've done business with them in the past, say:

> **"...depending on your needs, I'd like to find out if we can help you again?"**

If they say no, ask them why they stopped ordering or stopped using your product/service. Here's what I say when I call one of my customers back who hasn't been active or stopped buying.

> **"Hello Jim? This is Joe Catal with ABC Corp. We're the people who produced your telephone on-hold message program last year. Most companies go through some changes during the year, and I'm calling to see if we can update your program at a substantial discount. Do you have a moment to talk?"**

I like to add a benefit, the substantial discount. Do what you can to get these accounts active again.

Up-Selling is Servicing

Once you make a sale, always try to sell add-ons. When a customer tells me to ship one of my on-hold message systems, I also tell him about our holiday program, and how we offer a discount when we ship it with their initial order. I've found that about 50%-60% of the people buy it! You're doing your customers a disservice by not telling them about your other products. Also, if they find out a few months later that they could have gotten a discount on a product or service you didn't tell them about, it makes you look bad. Remember, don't stop selling until they quit buying!

Sell Smaller Items After a Large Sale

Keep in mind, if you sell a product to someone for $500, they'll more than likely be a good candidate to up-sell them some smaller items. Example.

> **"Jim, a lot of our customers also purchase the extra widget with this type of order. It's only $35. Would you like me to include that for you?"**

The $35 dollars won't sound like much compared to the $500. When you buy a car the cost might be $20,000. If the salesperson says for an extra $250, you can have the deluxe stereo sound system, you'll more than likely say OK. The $250 doesn't sound like much compared to the 20 grand. However, it will very rarely work if you try to sell low first, then high.

Don't Get Greedy

In Jim Domanski's book, *"Add-On Selling,"* he says to never try upselling other products or services until you've taken the order for the first product. If you start mentioning all types of other products, they'll just get confused. As a general rule, your add-ons should not be more than 25% of the original purchase price. If something cost $100, your add-on should not be more then $25.

23

Opening Statements Revisited

Earlier in the book I spoke about two types of opening statements; product and benefit statements. I would say most sales reps use one of these types of openings. I strongly recommend a third type of opening which I feel is the most powerful. It's the curiosity opening.

Here are some sobering statistics I've collected when calling business-to-business. On the average, when making 100 calls, my hit rate is around 5%. A hit is considered giving a presentation to the person I'm trying to reach. Giving presentations to receptionists don't count. The techniques in this book will help you make more sales, however, if your hit rate is still 5%, you can't expect to double your income. The key is to give more presentation to more qualified buyers.

What if I told you that you could give a presentation to 50% of the people you spoke to. Would you believe me? Probably not. The fact is, there are people like myself giving presentations to 50-80% of all the people they talk to. That's right, 50-80%!

In Michael T. Bosworths book *"Solution Selling,"* he explains why curiosity should be the foundation of your opening, and how you can double, triple, or even quadruple the amount of presentations your giving by getting people to tell you they want to hear more. I personally use Michael's method, and can tell you it works. He has four points that are important to crafting his type of opening.

1. **Make sure you can get through your opening in approximately twenty seconds**

2. **Seek only to gain one thing. Curiosity.**

3. **Think of a problem the buyer is likely to have.**

4. **Be prepared for a positive response.**

Here's Mike's template I've adapted from the book, with a couple of examples. You might think this seems a little long, but the results are outstanding.

> **"This is Joe Smith with** (company). **We've been working with the** (industry) **for the past** (#) **years. One of the chief concerns we're hearing from other** (job title) **is their *frustration* with** (critical issue). **We've been able to help our customers deal with this issue, and I'd like an opportunity to share with you how."**

Here's how it looks in a normal format.

> **"Tom, my name's Jim Johnson with ABC Computer Systems. We've been working with the toy industry for the past four years. One of the chief concerns we're hearing from other business owners, is their frustration because manufacturing is unable to fulfill all the sales orders written by their salespeople, causing them to lose valuable shelf space to their competition. We've been able to help our customers deal with this issue and I'd like an opportunity to share with you how."**

As you can see, he's talking about a critical issue that people in his industry have. What business owner wouldn't want to find out how other people in his industry are solving that problem? This is called the "herd theory." As a rule people tend to follow other people. It's very powerful.

No matter what type of product or service you sell, you have to realize that the person you're calling has probably been called six or more times about your type of offer. Have you ever called someone who told you they weren't interested in your offer, and when you called back six months later they purchased it from someone else? The main reason is because someone creative showed them a *different angle* about the product or service that made them think, and take action.

163

Earlier I said that no matter what you sell, it likely solves some type of problem for people. It generates extra income, saves time, etc. And, every industry has a critical problem that they want to solve.

Here's the opening statement I use that has given me a solid 60-65% hit (presentation) rate. Let's say I'm calling a mortgage company. I know for a fact that their biggest problem is having people call up to ask about their rates, and then go elsewhere to get their mortgage. 95% of all mortgage companies have this problem, and most business owners want to solve it. The idea is to develop an opening that addresses this issue so the people on the other end of the phone will want to talk to me. With the on-hold messages I sell, I know they cross-market products, keep people on-hold longer, and inform them that they don't need to shop around because the mortgage company they're calling can handle all their needs. Put yourself in the shoes of an owner of a mortgage company. Let's say I was calling you, and you heard this.

"Hello Jim? This is Joe Catal calling from American Systems. Jim, we've been working with the mortgage industry for the past 5 years, and one of the chief concerns we hear from other business owners, is their *frustration* with people who call in that are *shopping around*, and then go elsewhere for their mortgage. We've been able to help over one thousand mortgage companies deal with this problem, and the purpose of the call is to get your *personal* opinion on our service to see if it's something that might be able to help you. Do you have a moment to let me know?"

You better believe he wants to know! 60%-70% of the people I talk to will ask me what it is. *That's exactly what I want to hear.* If you were that business owner wouldn't you want to know how all those other people in your same industry are dealing with that problem? I personally don't like to use the word "share." I've found that asking people for their opinion is very powerful. If someone asks you for your opinion on something, you'll normally give it. The reason some people tell me they are not interested is because they may get their loans from a contractor, so people don't call to shop around.

Since I'm looking for a company that gets lots of calls from the public, he wouldn't qualify. As a sales person, we think everyone qualifies for our offer, but that's simply not true.

Analyzing this Technique

Lets dissect this opening for a moment. I know for a fact that the people I'm calling about my offer have been contacted at least six or more times. I know that 95% of the reps calling are using the product- or benefit-opening. The business owners I call don't want to buy an on-hold program. Instead I'm selling them a solution to a major problem they have. Since this is a different angle they may not have thought about, they'll now seriously look at this.

Most reps call up and want to play the person a sample, or tell them how it generates money. They hear that from everyone. Once they tell me they want to know more, I ask them if they're a full service mortgage company that can get loans for people with good-to-bad credit, or if they work in a niche market. Once they tell me, I go into my presentation, and once I play them the sample, they begin to see that having a program starts to make sense, even though they were against it when the last rep called. You see, you have to address their critical issue. *Business owners don't care about your product or how it works.* They're trying to find ways to relieve their problems. Also, when saying the word "frustration," make it sound a little painful to them. Emphasize it a little bit.

I also qualify him right up front with my first couple of questions. Not everyone I call qualifies for my offer, so I let them know. I don't want to get into a long dragged out reason why, but if you use this type of opening, qualify them right away with your first couple of questions. You don't want to give full presentations to people who wouldn't qualify for your offer. If you were selling insurance to companies with twenty or more employees as your target market, your first question might be,

"Jim, does your company have twenty or more employees?"

If yes, great. If he tells you it's a two-man operation, you can just tell him that your service wouldn't be for him, and move on.

Understanding Their Critical Issues

Top sales reps change with the times. During the next couple of years companies in my industry will be closing their doors at a rapid pace. In fact, they've already started. They've been selling their product the same way for years. The market is getting saturated, and they can't keep up with the competition. The funny thing is our company is continually growing! In fact, just this past year we've shown a 40% increase in sales, and were looking to expand again!

In order to find out what the critical issues might be for your industry, you can read trade journals, or go to their association website to see issues they talk about. You can even call one of your existing customers and ask them. Just tell them what you're doing, and let them know you wanted to get their personal opinion. They'll be flattered and will help you. Also, if you're calling executives, instead of saying business owners in your opening, say executives. Tailor it to the person you're talking to.

I want to point something out. A lot of you out there might be thinking that everyone knows if you generate curiosity, people will want to talk to you. That's true. However the element that's missing is the *critical issue.* I could just call up and say,

"Hi Jim, this Joe Catal with American Systems. Jim, we've been working in the mortgage industry for the past 5 years helping business owners generate extra business. And I'd just like to get your personal opinion on our service to see if it's something that might be able to help you. Do you have a moment to let me know?"

I've tried things similar to this, and have gotten a good response, but since I wasn't bringing up that critical issue, I didn't write as much business. The key is the critical issue. Stick to the original format.

What if the person tells you they're not interested or they don't have that problem? You have two choices. One, you can say thank you and good-bye, (which is what I do). Two, you mention a second critical issue. For the example I used, I could say,

"Would you like to know how other people in your industry are cross marketing their products to generate extra business?"

166

Do what you feel is comfortable for you. Since I have such a high presentation rate, I just move on. Also, If you know someone's critical issue and they wouldn't even be curious as to how other people solved it, don't you think that would be a hard sell? Just move on.

Using Fronters

Another point I'd like to bring up is the use of fronters. These are people who prospect for you. These people are generally used for volume dialing. Once the fronter gives the opening and asks a couple of questions up front to qualify the person, they could say something like, Irv, our service/product could apply to your situation. Real quickly I'm going to put my office manager on, and she'll be able to quickly explain what we do. Here's Susan, Irv. When you have fronters you may want to use the product/benefit opening we discussed earlier in the book. I like my fronters to make 30-40 calls an hour. I personally use them for volume dialing. You can experiment with the openings you want your fronters to use.

I always like to look at opening statements. If you use the curiosity opening, send it to me. I'll look at it for you and critique it. Of course if you're a competitor, you're on your own! Now that you know how to increase your hit rate by using curiosity, you'll see your sales start to increase dramatically. Keep track of how many contacts you make, and how many presentations you give. If it's less than 50%, you may not be addressing the right critical issue. When I say contacts, I mean the actual person you're trying to reach who says tell me more. Let me know how you're doing!

You can also use the curiosity opening for voice mail, e-mail, faxing, and answering machines. Just make sure at the end of your message you leave a time when they can reach you.

Note: Earlier in the book I said you should be making 30-40 calls an hour. Of course if you make contact with four people during that hour who have an interest in your offer, you may only have made ten calls. That's ok. The 30-40 an hour is if you're not making contact. You should just fly through your leads until you get the person you want.

24

More on Qualifying And Presenting

I can't stand it when I hear the phrase "Buyers are liars." To me, a buyer is a liar who tells you to ship his product COD and doesn't accept the package. That's a legitimate liar. The reason why so many sales people think buyers are liars is they don't qualify their prospects well enough. The real statement should be, "Some buyers seem like liars because the person trying to sell to them is a bad qualifier."

It not the customer's fault if he keeps putting you off and you're calling back 50 times to get an order. Very few salespeople call a prospect back and ask for the order! I hear stupid things like "What do you think?" "How are things going?" "Are you ready to go ahead?" Quit the baby talk and ask for the order! If you keep calling people back who won't buy, it's not the customer's fault, it's yours.

Here are a few examples I use to qualify prospects. I want you to keep in mind, that you should only be calling back "high probability" people. When you hang up the phone, ask yourself this: On a scale from 1-10, what would you rate the customer? If it's less than an 8, don't consider them a high probability prospect. I make between 100-150 calls a day, and have between 20-30 call backs at any given time. If you have more call backs than that, you're not qualifying people.

I'll also let you know that my callback conversion rate is around 40-50%. The reason is because I simply ask them when I call back if there would be any reason they wouldn't be able to give me an order. Once they start hemming and hawing, I leave my number and I'm on to the next prospect. Be brutal in your qualification process. It's been proven over and over that sales people are the weakest in the qualifying area. Unless I'm working on a huge account, I know it takes one-to-three calls to close my sale. I NEVER call someone back more than three times. Here are a few samples of how I weed out high probability prospects from low probability ones.

"I'm Getting a New Phone System"

People who want a telephone on-hold message program need a phone system. A lot of people tell me to call them back because they really want what I have. Since they're not qualified at this time, I ask them these questions to see if it even warrants a call back.

"Have you chosen a phone vendor yet?"

"Have you decided on the brand you want?"

If he says no to these questions, he's not a callback because he's a low probability sale. If he tells me he's having a vendor come out within 30 days, I say:

"If the price is right and you like what they show you, are you going to buy the new system now, or wait until a later date?"

If he says he'll buy it, I ask him if he'll still be able to fit this into his budget. I also try and get the order today. I'll tell him it will take a few weeks to get the finished product, and he can have it there when they come out to set the new system up. This will save him $50 on having them come out again on a service call. If he says no to that, I know when I call back my chances are slim.

If you have customers telling you they're getting new computer systems installed, or some other changes, find out how far along they've gotten. If they haven't started, move on. Don't lie to yourself thinking you have a great prospect for next year. You're looking for people who want what you have, and can afford it NOW! Not next year.

"I Have a Partner"

This is another lame excuse I hear every day. If he has a partner, I ask him if his partner's in so I can play him the sample and answer any of his questions. If the partner is not in, I ask him when I should call back to speak with him so I can play him the sample and answer any of his questions. If he doesn't give me access to his partner, he's a low probability prospect. This is not a call back, and not worth sending info to. *NOTE:* If you're working on a large account, you may not talk with the CEO. Just make sure you find out if the CEO has to sign off on your offer. If so, make sure the CEO has agreed to go ahead with it. If they don't pay by credit card, make sure the person you're talking with has the CEO OK the approval form. As salespeople, you have to be able to let go! If they don't want to follow you through your selling process, it's over. It's really that simple.

Calling Their Vendor

If I'm not sure about the phone system, I tell them I need to talk to their phone vendor about the compatibility of their system. If he won't let me talk to his vendor, he's a low probability prospect. What serious buyer wouldn't want to know if he could even implement our system?

"We'll Do It After the Holiday."

This is a lame excuse. If you absolutely have to call back after a holiday, say,

"So if I understand you correctly, when I call you back mid-January, you'll give me your order?"

If he says yes, say,

"Between now and then, do you see anything that would keep you from going ahead with this?"

If he says he has to see, or has to check his budget, or that he don't know, you have a low probability prospect. **Get an absolute yes.** If they can't commit to you, make ONE call back in January and ask for the order. If he gives you a no, toss it! Serious prospects don't care about holidays. If they want what you have, they'll buy it any time of the year.

And while we're on the subject of holidays, don't use that as an excuse that it's a bad time to sell. Only amateurs do that. The real pros tighten up their belts and go all out swinging. They prospect more, and get more aggressive. Since I'm in the advertising business, the month of December is considered a bad month to sell. I don't see any difference in my sales than any other month. I normally take my vacation the 25th of December thru the 1st of January. Other than that, the holidays really don't make a difference. You need to have that kind of mindset. And it comes from prospecting and qualifying people the right way.

Also, the week before I leave for vacation, I call all my customers to wish them happy holidays, and if they need to update their program, to give me a call after the 1st. If the person is not in, I leave a voice mail. If they don't have voice mail, I have a "Happy Holiday" letter I fax to them. If you have your customer's e-mail address, you can e-mail them. When I get back from vacation, I usually have a number of people who have called to update their program. It's a great way to start the new year.

If You Must Send Info ...
Try this to determine if it's worth sending something.

"Jim, from what I've explained to you today along with the info I'll be sending you, if everything checks out and is to your liking, would there be anything you can think of that would keep you from going ahead with this when I call you back after the holiday?"

This will weed out any further objections and let me know if he's worth faxing and following up on. Don't send info for no reason. The literature doesn't do the selling for you. Qualifying your customer does. Earlier in the book, I included a call back script. USE IT!

There will be times when you have to use your gut feeling. Just keep in mind, if you have more than 35 callbacks at any one time, you're really not qualifying people well enough. Also keep in mind that when you call a customer back and he tells you he's not interested, he's telling you the truth! At least he's not stringing you along with a maybe. When I have to call a person back, I always tell them when I call back I'll be asking them for their order. Would there be anything that would keep them from giving me a yes or no at that time?

Presentation Dissection
Here's a technique that will improve your closing ratio dramatically. For those of you who have to train sales people, this will be a godsend to make your life easier. No matter what you sell, your presentation can be broken down into *sections*. It can be two sections, or it can be 10. With the on-hold systems I sell, I have three sections of my presentation that can be broken down.

171

1. The technical aspect. How to hook the player into your phone system.

2. How we work. Writing the scripts, edits, produce, etc.

3. Pricing.

Each of us starts our presentation a certain way, and then moves on. In reality, your presentation can be broken down into chunks. Here's an example. Let's assume I'm past my opening and the prospect wants to hear more about my offer. The first thing I'll cover is the technical side of how it works.

> **"Mr. Prospect, right now you're playing music through your phone lines. That tells me you have a phone system and can do this. To play messages on-hold, all you need to do on your end is just change out your radio for a boom box CD player, and you are ready to go. Right now you have your radio plugged into your main phone box somewhere in your office. There's a small wire running from your system to the earphone jack of that radio. All you do is take that same wire you have in your radio, and plug it into the earphone jack of the CD player, and you're ready to go. *Any questions about the hook-up you may not be sure about?"***

I don't want to bore you with a full blown technical dissection, I just want you to see how I end the first section. ("Any questions about the hook-up you may not be sure about?").

Always remember, you can NEVER successfully move to the next section of your presentation until the person fully understands the section you're on. In my industry, most reps would have just told the prospect since he's playing the radio, he's compatible. What does "compatible" mean to the customer? I can't just assume because I know how it hooks up, that he does. Years ago when I was interested about learning about the Internet I received several calls from companies trying to get me to sign up. I didn't really know much about it, and was afraid of making a bad decision. When people called they'd just tell me that because I have a phone line, I could easily be on the Internet. They'd then just tell me how great it was. I had a lot of questions to ask. For example, if I e-mail my sister in California, would I get a long distance charge?

If I went to someone's website, would I have to pay? Sales reps just assumed I knew how the net worked, when I didn't have a clue.

Maybe you don't sell a product that needs a technical hook-up, but it doesn't matter. Let's say you sold life insurance. There are different types, and it would be in your best interest to give a brief overview of the differences. Then ask if they have any questions about the different types. The more you educate your prospect, the more of an intelligent decision they'll make.

On to Section 2 of the presentation. Once they thoroughly understand how the hook-up works, I'll explain how we work.

> **"Mr. Prospect, the way we write a script for your company is by me taking a few minutes with you to ask you some questions about it. When the script is finished—which takes about a week—we'll call you back and review it with you. At that time ...** *Do you have any questions about that part of it you may not be sure about?"*

If he has a question, I'll answer it and say,

> **"Does that answer your question?"**

As you can see, by asking this question after each section, I'm closing doors. Once a customer understands, they won't bring that issue up later.

Finally, Section 3 of the presentation, covering pricing.

> **"Mr. Prospect, as far as our pricing goes, it's pretty straight forward. There are no monthly or yearly fees, and no contracts to lock into. It's just a simple one-time investment of just $499 and you own it outright. If you ever decide you want to change your messages, future updates and changes are only $249. And the CD comes with a lifetime warranty. If it ever wears out or breaks, just send it back to us and we'll replace it for free.** *Any questions about the pricing structure you may not be sure of?"*

Once the customer says he doesn't have any questions, or I've answered any he has, I'll say:

173

"Jim, there's really nothing more to it than that. You sound to me like you understand everything there is to know about this. Would you like us to show you what we can do for you?"

I'd like to mention a few things here. First you might have noticed I didn't ask any other questions throughout this presentation. I actually do, but I didn't want to bore you with the technical details of my business. I just wanted to get my point across: Never go to the next section of your presentation until you know the person's confident he understands the section you're on.

Look at your presentation and break it down into sections. Then place the sentence; **"Are there any question about that you may not be sure of?"** after it.

Another important point is that there may be *mini*-presentations inside of a single section. As an example, with my product, the technical side of hooking it up may have several options.

1. They might be playing a radio through their phone lines.

2. They may already have the CD player.

3. They may not be playing anything, and I'll have to explain where the music jack is on their phone system.

4. They may not have a music jack in their system, and I'll have to call their phone vendor.

5. They may have a digital unit.

Each and every one of these mini-presentations will have to be explained in detail, in their own individual way. Each one needs to be scripted out. For those of you who have to train salespeople to sell, this makes your life easier. The first thing I do is teach them the first part of the presentation, which is the technical part. I won't teach them the other two sections until they've mastered the first. It simply doesn't make sense. That means they'll have to study on their own time. (God forbid!). If they're not willing to do that, they won't be a good closer. Some people may take a few days, others a month. But it's important you let them know, they can't advance to the next section of learning the script until they become an expert at the first part. Even if someone tells me they have 10 years experience, I don't care, I take them through this process.

I've been using this technique and training people this way for a number of years, and can tell you, this is an extremely powerful technique. I've seen low produces go from two sales a week, up to five, six and seven almost over night. Your customers love it when you ask them if they have any questions they may not be sure about. It's showing them that you want them to fully understand.

If you're addressing a group, you could say,

"Does anybody in the group have any questions about this part of it they may not be sure of ?"

Once you answer their question, ask them if that answered their question. Then say **"Does anybody else have any questions about this part of it I can answer for them?"** This makes you come off as such an expert. (Which you are).

Questions are the Key

Over the years many people have asked me if there is any one technique that I think makes top producers successful. In one single word the answer is *questions.* The best salespeople are the ones who know how to ask great questions, and get the prospect involved. Many people think it's building a relationship. That's partially true, but by asking good questions, the relationship will automatically form. I'm not talking any type of questions, I'm talking well thought out questions with the prospect's interest in mind.

Another quick point I want to make is that with the above question you learned to ask after each section, you don't have to say it exactly the same way each time. You'll notice on my technical part, I said:

"Any question about the *hook up* you may not be sure about?"

With pricing I said *pricing* you may not be sure of?

For those of you who have scripts already written out, look at them and draw lines where you go from one section to the next. Incorporate the above question after each section, and start using it right away. You'll see immediate results. For others, write out your script and break it down. If someone in your same industry is using the above technique and you're not, there's no way you can compete with them. Also, make sure when you finish the *last* section of your presentation, you remember to ask if they have questions about it! From my years of experience training people, they want to just go directly into asking for the order. Don't get caught in that trap. The great thing about this technique is that it doesn't add any extra time to your presentation. It's just a simple sentence that packs a wallop. NOW USE IT!

25

Getting Commitment

Never, never, never, accept a **verbal** agreement by phone without the other person doing something. Never! The only time would be if you've been doing business with someone for a long time, and built a solid relationship.

You or your company's cancel rate should not be more than 20%. Here's how to handle the situation. First, you want to make sure you're dealing with the decision maker. As I said earlier, when you buy or search for prospect leads, find ones with the C.E.O., president, or owner's name on them.

After taking their order, ask them if there are any other questions they have before you hang up. Then say,

    "Great." Now to get started all I need is a credit
☞ **card. Which one would you like to put it on?"**

If they give you the credit card, you have a solid deal. Depending on what you're selling, this may not be applicable. So here are more ideas.

If they tell you they feel uncomfortable giving you their card number, just tell them you like to get some type of commitment from them. After all, you are going to work for them. Ask them if half now, and half on delivery would be fair to them. Try and get money. Cash. Dollars!

If at that point they still won't commit to that (and my experience says 50% won't), do this:

Tell them you understand how they feel about giving you their credit card number. Tell them you'll fax them an "Approval Form." They just need to "OK" it and fax it back to you.

When you fax it over, call right back and review it with them. You want it back right away! If a day goes by and they them. You want it back right away! If a day goes by and they haven't sent it, you may not have a serious prospect, or they have a partner that they are not telling you about. If a week goes by and they haven't faxed it back, make one more call and say,

> **"Jim, a week ago you told me you were going to fax back the approval form, and I still haven't received it. Is there still something you're not sure about?"** Or,

> **" Jim, a week ago you told me you were going to fax back the approval form, and I still haven't received it. Are you going to follow through with this, or are we finished talking?"**

Sure it's direct. But you'll definitely get an answer. Use whichever one you feel is necessary. If they don't fax it back, you saved yourself a cancel and a potential chargeback. If you can't get a commitment, don't turn your order in.

The approval form is very psychologically powerful, and I find very few people ever cancel when they send it back. Make sure it's easy to read. Don't put your fax number in the middle of a sentence. Have it stand out on its own.

Once your order is ready to ship, and the customer sees you've done your work, many will use their credit card. If they don't want to do that, send it C.O.D. I'm not big on invoicing someone unless we've established a relationship already.

But what if he says he's uncomfortable with a C.O.D. because he's not sure he'll get what he wants? Say,

> **"Bob, if you receive your order and it's not exactly what we agreed to, you can call your bank and put a stop payment on your check. Do you really think we went through all this work to get your business just so you would do that?"**

This gets them to think rationally, and 99% of the people will accept the C.O.D. I also let them know if there's a problem for any reason, call me directly, and I'll handle it personally.

ABC Company
123 West Street
Anytown, USA 12345

Approval

January 20, 2002
To: Pat Dillon
Quality Industrial

From: Terry Canton

WE NEED YOUR *OK* TO GET STARTED!

ABC Corp. will write and produce a custom computer program for you accounting department. In order for us to get started, there are only two requirements.

1. You alone are the sole decision maker or, any other decision makers have *all* agreed to go ahead with this project.

2. Your custom program is a one-time investment of $5,000. Upon program approval, there would be nothing to keep you from purchasing the program.

If the above requirements are satisfactory, please OK below and **FAX BACK TO: 1-222-222-2222**

Your OK_____

We thank you for your order, and look forward to a long term relationship with you.

KEEP IT THAT SHORT AND SIMPLE!

More on C.O.D.'s

Anytime you send a C.O.D., fax them an invoice. Don't depend on their memory. As soon as you fax it, call back and tell the receptionist you just faxed an invoice to Susan, and to make sure it gets to her desk, because she's expecting it. Keep it short and simple so they can read it at a glance. Here's a good sample to use.

ABC Corp.

1-800-000-0000

January 28, 2002

To: Susan Smith
Energy Advisors

C.O.D. SHIPPING INFORMATION

Your computer program will arrive
Monday, February 4, 2002

Please have a company or personal check made out to:

A.B.C. Corp.

in the amount of $5000.00.

We thank you for your business and look forward to a long- term relationship with your company. We wish you many more years of success and good health.

To really tighten this up, you can have the decision maker sign it and fax it back before you ship the product.

If someone won't sign off on your C.O.D. form, what's the liklihood they'll accept the package?

If you're working with a manager, make sure the real decision maker signs it, not the manager. If someone does sign it, and refuses the package, you're dealing with a real dead beat. Don't do any type of business with them. They'll send you bad checks, and dispute the credit card charges.

26

Selling On Inbound Calls

When someone calls into your company inquiring about your services, you need to know how to handle the call. Here are some ideas and tips that will give you an idea of what you need to do.

First, let's look at my inbound script.

"Hello, Joe speaking. How may I help you."

Customer: "I'm calling to get information about your on-hold programs."

Me: "Who am I speaking to?"

Customer: "My name's John Smith."

Me: "John, in case we disconnected, what number can I call you right back at?" (Get a name and a number).

Customer: "It's 900-123-4567."

Me: "John, are you the owner of the company?" (I ask this right up front, no games)

Customer: "Yeah." (If it's a manager, you'll probably have to send the info)

Me: "John, in order to play messages on-hold, you need to have a phone system that can play music through your phone lines. Are you playing anything on-hold now?" (Qualifying them right away)

Customer: "Yeah, we play the radio."

Me: "That tells me you have a phone system and can do this. What does your company do?"

Customer: "We sell all types of insurance."

Me: "How did you hear about us?"

Customer: "I heard your program over at Mortgage Corp."

Me: "What was it you liked about it?

Customer: "I liked the way it talked about the different programs they offered."

Me: "Why are you considering a program like this for your company?" (always ask this question on an in-bound call, ALWAYS!)

Customer: "A lot of our customers don't know all the types of insurance products we offer, and we think this would be a good way to let them know."

Me: "Do you think some of your customers are purchasing one type of insurance from you, and going else where for their other insurance products because they don't know all that you offer?" (Bringing up a problem with an implication)

Customer: "Yeah, that's the problem."

Me: "John, we've worked with other people in your industry who've had a similar problem. Let me tell you how we work and go over the pricing with you."

At that time I give him my presentation and ask for the order or set the appointment.

Keep in mind, when you advertise and have people call in, you need to know what you're trying to accomplish. Are you trying to make a sale, set an appointment, or send info? This should be your only focus and goal on an inbound call. They wouldn't be calling if they weren't interested. If you're selling a complicated high-ticket item, and you have to send info, make sure someone follows up! It doesn't make sense to send info and not follow up. That's just plain idiotic in my mind.

For those of you who don't sell a complicated product and can close the sale on one call, ask for the order. *Ask for the order!* **Ask for the order!**

If your company sends info out, make sure people follow

up! I get a ton of info in the mail from infomercials and ads I call about, but very rarely does someone call me to ask about it. They just assume I'll call. It's your job to follow up.

If you don't have an inbound script developed, don't bother advertising. You're just wasting your money. Better yet! Send *me* the cash!

And, if they're calling to place an order, make sure you try and upsell them. Tell them about add ons.

Tips for Selling on the Inbound Call

Here are a collection of brief tips to help you turn more of those incoming calls into cash.

Have an "Assume the Sale" Attitude

On an inbound call, have an "assume the sale attitude." Don't make the mistake of blabbing how great your company is, until you know why they need your services. With the proper script, and talking to the decision maker, you should be able to close or set appointments for 70% of your inbound calls. This number is very realistic. Of course if you're taking orders from an infomercial or TV commercial, it should be much higher. But since most of us aren't working for companies that advertise like that, the 70% number should be your goal. My personal success rate is right at 80%.

Have a System

Keep in mind that almost everyone who calls in will want you to send info. You need to have a systematic method of tracking your inbound calls. Make sure only qualified salespeople are talking with customers. Unless your receptionist is a trained sales person, don't have her answering questions or sending info to anyone. Also, make sure your script enhances their problem once you ask the "Why are you considering...?" question. Apply pain, pain, pain, add salt, and twist the knife! Then offer the solution. More often than not, they'll give you the order

Note: I personally believe that not all sales people should take inbound calls. Make them earn it! Only have your best players on the team handle them. No third stringers. Also, while I'm on the subject, just because someone has worked at your company for a while, doesn't mean they get more privileges than the others. If he/she's a sales person, they have to earn their keep. No free loaders.

Ask Why They Called

When someone calls in from a brochure, commercial, or radio ad, ask them what they liked about it.

"What was it that caught your attention?"

Their answer will give you a good idea of what they're looking for.

Another Great Question

On an inbound call, here's a killer question to ask:

"Why are you considering something like this for your company? "

This question will get them talking about their problem. They'll spill their guts and tell you every thing you need to know. **"Why are you considering"** is one of the most powerful questions you can ask someone on an inbound call. Ask it every time.

Ask How Familiar They Are With You

Ask this early in the call:

"John, do you know very much about our company? "

Say it exactly that way. This gives you the chance to explain you've been in business 10 years, you have 20 offices, over 2,000 satisfied customers, 50 employees, and most of your business comes from repeat orders and referrals. That's better than saying, "Do you know who we are?" If he doesn't, he may feel stupid. Not a good way to start off.

What to Say to Referred Leads

If someone calls in from a referral, don't tell the person you sold John Smith your system, or that he buys from you all the time, etc. Tell them that,

"John's been using our service for 2 years, and he's been really happy with us. After shopping around, he found that we were the best value for his money."

That gets the point across.

They Called YOU!

When a person calls you from a referral or an ad, keep in mind they're being proactive. They initiated the selling process. People make changes when they've reached their threshhold of pain. You go on a diet because you can't take being overweight anymore. Once you understand that concept, you can close a lot more people. They more than likely have investigated your product or service. All you need to really do is give them the nudge to buy. Sell them on safety. All they want is a little reassurance that they're making the right decision. Keep that in mind! They just need someone to confirm what they already know. If you're talking to the decision maker, and they qualify for your offer, you should close 70% of these people. Have the mindset that they're calling to give you their business.

Get the Name and Number Early

Whenever getting an incoming call, always get their name and number.

"Joe, in case we get disconnected, what number can I call you right back at?"

If you do get disconnected, call right back. Don't wait for them to call you.

They'll Buy From Someone

I've seen statistics that state if someone calls your place of business about your product/service, whether they buy from you or not, 45% of those people will purchase that product/service within the next 12 months. That's why it's important to follow up every 3 months for one full year. You want to make sure they know who to call when they're ready to buy.

Be Careful With the Mysterious Call

If someone calls you out of the blue for a proposal, be leery. Ask if the company has already made a decision to use your service/product. Who else are they considering? What criteria will they use to make their choice? I'm always leery when people call me out of the blue. Are they a competitor? How did they hear about us?

Sell Them at their New Company

Occasionally an employee who worked at a company you sold your product to will quit and go to work for someone else. They'll call you and tell you they used your product or service at their other company. Ask them what they liked about the product/service. You'll close most of these types of sales.

When a Committee is Involved ...

If someone calls you and they have a problem and a definite need for your product/service, but still wants to run it by his group, say,

> **"If the group says no, what will you do in the future about the situation?"**

Owners can make their own decisions if they want to.

27

Taking Accounts From Competitors

Most sales reps run into situations where the prospect is already buying from a competitor. Here are some ideas on how to win that business.

Uncover the Pain Instead of Asking Them What They Like

When they say they are working with your competitor, don't ask them if they're happy with their current supplier. Instead, you need to apply a little pain. Here's what I mean. My on-hold messages are on a compact disc. I know that many of my competitors put them on cassettes. Cassettes wear out and break, CD's don't. So when I'm told they already have a program, I say **"Is that on cassette?"**

Knowing 75% of the time the answer will be yes, I then get them thinking about the pain:

> **"How many times a year do you have to replace those tapes from wearing out and breaking?"**

They'll say 2-3 times a year. I reply,

> **"Have you ever considered putting your program on a compact disc that never wears out or breaks, and comes with a lifetime warranty?"**

Most will tell me they haven't, and ask me how much it would be to do that. That's **exactly** what I want them to say. As you can see, this will get them thinking of a problem that I can solve. Every product or service has a weakness. If you can figure out how to exploit it, and you have the solution, you'll steal accounts.

Learn When Their Contract Expires

If someone is locked into a contract, ask them when it expires and how you go about putting in a bid. Send in your bid early. Ask who their current supplier is. Obtain their existing vendor's brochures, catalogs, or go to their web site and see what you're up against. Find a weakness that you can exploit and go for it. Of course if you're into volume dialing like me, this would be a lot of work, and may not be realistic.

Learn Why They're Changing

Sometimes a prospect will tell you they're looking to change vendors. Before babbling on about how great your company is, you have to find out why they want to change. What would they like to have that they're not getting now? I actually say,

"So I don't make the same mistake as your other vendor, what is about them that you're not happy with?"

This really opens the door for you. Maybe they're always late on deliveries. Find out how often they need deliveries. Maybe they can't keep them supplied on a regular basis. Find out how much of a supply they need. Make sure you know why they're looking to change vendors so you don't make the same mistake.

Ask for 1%

Here's a phrase you may be able to work into your arsenal. Sometimes people are hesitant to do business with you. Maybe you're out of state, or they're not familiar with your company. Just tell them all you want is 1% of their trust/business, and an opportunity to earn the other 99%.

28

Tips for Outside Sales Reps

As you probably have concluded already, most of the ideas I've covered here are also applicable to outside sales reps. Here are some specifically for reps who also see customers face-to-face.

Confirming Appointments

Tom Hopkins has a great opening when calling people back for an appointment.

If you have to confirm an appointment, don't call up and say I'm just calling to make sure you'll be there tonight at 6 o'clock. Instead, say,

"Mr. Smith, I'm calling to let you know I've put a lot of time and effort into your proposal, and I think you'll really be excited about what I've come up with for you. I'll be there at six o'clock, and I just wanted to make sure my directions are right."

This develops interest and curiosity so the prospect will want to see what you have. You're not calling up to see if they'll be in. Understand the concept, and work it to fit your situation. For example, when I call people back to let them know their on-hold message script is ready, I tell them I just finished reading their script and it's a knockout, and that I'm going to have someone from our production department call them back to review it with them. I want to get them excited, and in the mood to want to hear it.

Appeal to All of the Senses

If you go out on face-to-face presentations, keep in mind your prospect has five senses. Hearing, touch, sight, taste and smell. Appeal to as many of those senses as you can, and you'll have an extra edge.

When Selling in the Home ...

When going on outside appointments to a residence, *don't* ring their doorbell. Knock instead. The reason is that they may have small children sleeping and you'll wake them up. Do you want to give your presentation to someone with screaming kids in their arms? It's little things like this that make you succeed.

You should also give your presentation in the kitchen, not the living room. *Friends* sit in kitchens and talk. The living room is for business. If you have to give your presentation in a restaurant, get there early and find a table that keeps your prospect from facing all the people. You want them to be focusing on you, not the other people around you. It's even better if they're facing you with a wall behind you.

You're <u>Always</u> on an Appointment

If you have to leave the office for any reason, always tell the receptionist to tell your customers you're on an outside appointment. Let the receptionist know when you'll be back. If it's an emergency call, have the receptionist page you. Make sure the receptionist never says things like he's still at lunch, I don't know when he'll be back, etc. You're **always** on an appointment with a customer. Also, when giving a face-to-face presentation, leave your pager and cell phone in the car. Think about the impression you make when you stop in the middle of a presentation to take a call. No one is more important to you than the people you're giving your presentation to.

Bring an Article

If you go out on appointments, a good ice breaker to start a conversation is to bring an article about their industry. A good article would be about a problem in their industry. Ask them about it. Is it a problem for them? Have they solved it? People like to talk about their industry. This is really an excellent technique. It's a lot better than looking at their kid's pictures and making small talk.

Clean Your Briefcase

Make sure your briefcase is neat and organized. You don't want to open it up and have papers falling out of it. BE ORGANIZED!

A Presentation Approach

Here's a technique people use who give face to face presentations. I personally like this direct approach. See if you can mold it into your presentation.

> **"Mr. Piggy, my name's Susan Smith. I work for ABC Corp. I promise I won't try to sell you anything. All I'm going to do is tell you why other people bought, or how other people in your same situation increased sales, saved time, etc. If it makes sense to you and can fit into your budget, then try it/ buy it, if not, then don't buy it. Is that fair enough?"**

Although this is direct, it's also a soft sell. What person would say no to that? Remember, they agreed to seeing you. This opening gets them to relax a little.

I especially like the phrase,

> **"If it makes sense to you and can fit into your budget, buy it. If not, don't buy it."**

No matter what you sell by phone, you can work that into your arsenal. You can say something like,

> **"Mr. Smith, if you have a moment I'd just like to ask you a few quick questions to see if this could be of any value to you. If it makes sense and can fit into your budget we'll talk. If not, I promise I'll let you get right back to work. Fair enough?"**

192

29

Last Resort Techniques

Here's an idea I learned from a friend in the collections industry. I told him I was having some problems with people not getting back to me for work we've already done for them. He told me about a "final notice" letter that will give you a 90% response. The letter is to be used as a last resort. If I've left repeated messages and voice mails over a three-week period and still haven't heard back, I know there's a problem. No matter what product or service you sell, it has a time limit when the deal should go through. With my industry, it's around three weeks. In the case of someone not calling back to review the scripts with him, I send the letter shown on the following page.

This is a brutal letter to send, but it gets the job done. Let's break it down. The beginning lets the customer know we've made numerous attempts to get him to call. If people won't return your calls, this is a bad sign. We then tell him to call to schedule a time that's convenient to him. Since people may be busy, this is a logical approach. We also let him know that he can call anytime and we'll make time for him. Now he has an opportunity to call from a cell phone if he has to. We let him know he's only ten minutes away from finishing the project. Who doesn't have ten minutes to spend with someone if they knew this would improve their business?

We then get aggressive. We want a response one way or the other. We'll tell them we're shipping the program in its present form. We also let them know if they can't meet the deadline, we'd like to get half of the payment for the work we've done. If someone was serious about following through, they'd do it. And notice the key phrase at the very end. *"Please understand that we will proceed as agree unless you call and*

ABC Corp.
1-800-000-0000

January 28, 2002
To: Susan Smith
Energy Advisors

FINAL NOTICE

Several weeks ago you hired our firm to write a customized telephone on-hold message advertising script for your company. During the past three weeks, we've made several calls to schedule a day and time for us to review it with you, but don't seem to be getting anywhere.

Whether you know it or not, you're literally 10 MINUTES away from completing this project. Once we read the script back, you'll have the program in your hand a week later.

Since time is the only thing holding this up, we need to schedule a date and time to review the changes with you. We're available Monday-Friday 9-5 eastern time. You do not need to schedule an appointment. You can call at your convenience, and we'll make time for you.

If we do not hear from you by the below date, we'll ship your program in its present form. If you need additional time, we'd like to get half the payment for the work we've already done, and the balance upon shipping. This would show us some commitment on your end that you'll be following through with this in the near future. We accept all major credit cards.

WE NEED TO HEAR BACK FROM YOU BY March 25, 2002

Sincerely,
Pat Salesrep

make a change." This statement is common to see on collection notices. It's very intimidating.

You'll likely get one of these five responses:

1. They'll call and resolve the issue immediately.

2. They'll call to schedule an appointment.

3. They'll pay you half now and the balance upon shipping or approval.

4. They'll call and cancel.

5. They won't call. Which means they were never going to follow through anyway.

I also send a letter for people who've called for the read back, but asked us to fax the script so they can review it. The letter is exactly the same except for the beginning.

> **Several weeks ago we sent you a customized telephone on-hold message script we wrote for your company. We normally don't send our scripts out without payment, but we made an exception in your case. We've made several attempts to schedule a time to go over the changes with you, but don't seem to be getting anywhere.**
>
> **Since time is the only thing holding this up, we need to schedule a date and time to review the changes with you. We're available Monday-Friday 9-5 Eastern time. You do not need to schedule an appointment. You can call at your convenience, and we'll make time for you.**

Over the years I've found I've gotten a more positive response than negative. Here are a few tips on using it.

☐ Fax out all your letters on Fridays. This gives them the weekend and a full week to do what they have to do.

☐ When you fax the letter out, call the receptionist and let her know you sent a final notice to John Smith, and you want to make sure she puts it on his desk so he gets it. By using the words "final notice," she'll get to it right away. Most of the people will respond the same day.

☐ I've also found it's a good idea to have someone else

take the call. In my situation I have the person from production talk with them. If that's not your situation, be prepared. They'll either call to apologize, or call to tell you off.

❑ Be firm! You've given them enough time. Now get some commitment.

> **"Jim, I realize you need another month, so to show us some commitment on your end, lets put half on a credit card now, and the balance when we ship it, ok?"**

If they say no to that, move on. Tell him to call you when they're ready to move forward, and that you won't be contacting him again.

This letter is to get you a yes, no, or some type of payment, not another extension. You can also use these letters for people who owe you money, or anything else you need to get resolved. They work!

Collecting Bad Debts

Unfortunately, there are people out there who pay slow, or worse, try to stiff you.

A friend of mine in the collections industry gave me some good advice when trying to collect on a bad check, credit card, or any other way you to try to collect money. He said at first be nice. Then brutal!

If you're ever in a situation where you have to make a collection from someone, and they're not returning your calls or the receptionist is giving you the run-around. Tell her,

> **"John leaves me no alternative. My company has no choice but to take further action."**

When the receptionist asks, what do you mean? Say,

> **"I'm not at liberty to say. This is a matter between John and my company."**

Some people go as far as telling the receptionist that their company has no choice but to take further action against the owner and his *employees*. The words *"but to take further action"* are very powerful. It gets people thinking about lawsuits, court, etc. Any time someone owes you money, be very direct! If your company received a check that bounced, start the conversation like this:

> **"Hello Jack. This is Susan Jones over at ABC Corp. I know this isn't the type of call you like to get, but I'm calling to find out what you're going to do about the check you sent us that bounced, along with the $25 service charge?"**

That's it. Don't say anything else. He now has to fully explain himself. The idea is to try to work something out with the person. Maybe one of their delivery trucks broke down and cost $2000 to fix. Maybe you can split payments, or have him use a credit card. Always try to work something out first, before any type of threat. Ninety-nine percent of the people will work with you. It will also build a good relationship with the person. Although I don't know how much of a relationship you want to build with someone who bounces checks. These are very solid techniques.

A Real Shocker

For one difficult person who continually refused to return my calls, I went to the Internet and downloaded a copy of a subpoena. I put his name and state on it and filled it out I faxed it over with a letter that read,

"If I don't hear from you in 24 hours, I will file a subpoena with your local courthouse."

I've done this on several occasions and have had a return call from everyone.

30

Selling and Negotiating
(They're not the same)

You may be a great salesperson, but are you a professional negotiator?

The minute your customer asks you if you have a better price, you've gone from sales to negotiating. Don't confuse the two. When unions go on strike, peace talks go on, or a hostage situation arises, they don't send salespeople. They send in professionally-trained negotiators.

In Roger Dawson's great book, "Secrets of Power Negotiating for Salespeople," he gives salespeople some incredible insight. Whether you go out on appointments or do all your business by phone, this book's for you. Order it today! Here are some of Roger's insights. I personally use his techniques and can tell you my sales have soared.

❏ Rather than lower the cost of your product or service to be the cheapest in the market, raise your prices! This will give you room to negotiate and also raise the perceived value of your offer.

❏ When you make a cold call to someone and don't know them, give them your *wish price*. If you're selling something for $400, you may want to sell it for $500. What you'll find so unbelievable is that a lot of people will give you your wish price.

❏ Listen for the *flinch*, which is a surprised, perhaps negative response, such as, "OOOOoooo." After giving your price, if they don't seem surprised or shocked, you know you're in their price range.

198

❑ When negotiating price, instead of saying you can deduct $100, tell the person you can deduct $50. If you have to go down again, take off $25, then $15, than $10. Once a person realizes you're down to your last ten dollars, they'll realize you're at your bottom line. (Although it may be the real price you were going after anyway). Whatever your negotiating room, deduct it in four parts.

❑ If someone says you'll have to do better on price, ask them **"Exactly how much better?"** Don't toss out a number. It may be lower than what they were going to say.

❑ To stop people from grinding you, simply say, **"If I do that for you, what can you do for me?"** That will end the grinding.

I could literally go on and on about Roger's techniques but you really need to read the book to fully understand how to negotiate.

Knowing how to effectively negotiate will make you a fully-rounded sales pro. You really don't have much of a chance to get business from someone you're competing with if they know more about negotiating than you. Once you understand the concepts, there's no reason why you can't jack up your prices by 25%. Your sales volume will soar, and you don't have to worry about losing business because you can always come down in price if necessary. LEARN TO NEGOTIATE!!

31

Motivation and Attitude

One aspect of selling you absolutely have 100% control over is your attitude. Without a great attitude, which fuels your motivation, you're nothing. Here are some tips for keeping your attitude up and motivation high.

You are a CEO

As of today, stop thinking like an employee, and start thinking like a CEO. Employees watch the clock. CEO.'s stay until the job is done. If you want success, you have to work hard at it. Success is a choice. If you don't make a sale for the day, stay an extra hour and dial. Put the effort in. If you believe your success is from 9-5 Monday-Friday, you'll never get it. Ask yourself, do you put the time and effort in it takes to be successful?

A Rule to Follow

Here's a good rule to follow as a salesperson. Yesterday is a canceled check, today is a promissary note, and today's cash is all you have in your pocket. So spend it wisely.

How to Structure Pay Periods

If you're an owner or manager, structure your pay period so that it is motivating to your salespeople. Here's what I mean. Most phone rooms are set up so that whatever you sell this week, you'll get paid on the next Friday. If a rep has a bad week, they'll know they'll have to wait two weeks to get a good paycheck. This is a lot of financial stress for people and will effect their sales. The pay period should be Wednesday, through Tuesday. If a rep ships something on Tuesday (the last day of the pay period), he'll get paid for it that Friday (three days later). You can also start the week Thursday, and end it Wednesday of the next week. If something ships on Wednesday, you'll get paid for it two days later that Friday. This does several things. If they had a few bad days the week before, this gives them a chance to salvage it. This will also motivate them to show up for work Monday. As you know, most employees think like employees, and many like to take Mondays off. It also gives them a chance to use the weekend to get themselves together again, and prepared to come in Monday ready to go. If you have commissioned phone reps, put them on this pay schedule if you can. This simple concept will show you a substantial increase in sales. The Monday-Friday pay structure is the worst type of pay structure for commissioned phone reps.

Don't Complain

Are you a positive or negative minded worker? If you walk into work every day complaining about all your problems, you're a whiner. Nobody really cares about your personal problems anyway. Don't be a complainer and whiner—it shows what an amateur someone is. Go into work this week and make it a point not to complain about ANYTHING! Try it. Just take things as they come. Don't mention work or personal problems. If there is a problem, look for the positive and the solution. If someone starts complaining to you, cut the conversation short, and don't get caught up in their negativity. If you really hate the job you're at, leave! If not, quit your bitchin!

Who Gets the Most Sales?

Have you ever noticed the people who work the hardest seem to make all the sales? Why do you think that is? And, always keep improving your selling skills. The more you learn, the more you earn. That's a fact!

The "Synergy Effect"

Always be aware of the "synergy effect." That's when you work hard at things and sales seem to start coming out of the blue. Reorders start coming in. People who you spoke to months ago call to put in an order, etc. When you start putting the wheels of motion to work for yourself, things will automatically start supporting you for your efforts. Top producers know that if they put in extra effort, all those little things will come their way. The more you put into your sales, the more you'll get out of it.

Do One Thing Well

If you're selling a high ticket item that pays you a good commission, and you're working two jobs, it's because you're not a good closer, or for that matter, not a professional salesperson. If you worked your first job the right way, you'd be earning more, and wouldn't need a second job. That's a reality check.

Persistence Pays

Here's one trait all top producers have. They're PERSISTENT. They never stop prospecting, never stop asking for the order, always following up, etc. No matter how good your selling skills are, without persistence you're destined to fail. Persistence is different than annoying people or calling them back 20 times a day. It's having a goal and focus to believe in yourself and your product or service.

Be Indispensable

Become so good at your sales profession that your company will feel you're indispensable. Everyone's replaceable, but being indispensable is a lot better. I normally bring in 40-50% of all the revenue that comes into the company. That means every other salesperson is dividing the other money amongst themselves. If I leave or they let me go, the company loses almost 50% of their revenue. That means the managers and owners' standard of living will decrease by 50%. If your paycheck were suddenly cut in half, how would your life change? Of course this doesn't mean because you're a top producer you're exempt from the rules of the company. It means you have *more* responsibility to uphold the values of the company. Lying, stealing, or cheating customers will not be tolerated by anyone, and you'd have to be let go. Attend the meetings, give suggestions when asked, dress appropriately and get along with other people. Talk positively about the company when new employees start.

Sell Smarter

The new breed of top salespeople don't sell hard—they sell smart. Most companies with a sales force are divided in two. The top producers hang out with top producers, and the low producers hang out with low producers. Why is that? Because low producers whine about how bad everything is. The economy, leads, territory, etc. Top producers don't want to be around those types of negative people. They find ways to overcome those obstacles. If you're a low producer, I suggest you start becoming friends with top producers. Their successful attitudes will rub off, and in no time you'll be at the top with them. People who sell more than you know more than you. Pick their brain and find out what it is.

Focus on the Solution

Use the 99% solution rule. If you have a problem, acknowledge it. Then spend 99% of your time figuring out the solution, not 99% of your time dwelling on the problem itself. If you've ever watched the movie "Apollo 13" with Tom Hanks, you know what I mean. They had over 100 obstacles to overcome to survive. They acknowledged the problem, but dwelled on the solutions.

Determine Your Bare Minimum Goal

Here's a great motivator for salespeople. Take your checkbook out and go over your last six months of living expenses. Rent, mortgage, electric, gas, food, phone, pager, cell phone, water, car payments, insurance...everything. We're talking basic living expenses. Add them all up and multiply that by 12. Let's say your total living expenses are $25,000 a year. $25,000 divided by 52 weeks equals $480 a week. That's how much you need to make in order to just pay your bills. Now ask yourself how many sales a week you need to make to generate that income. Also keep in mind, this doesn't include saving money for trips, movies, and other fun activities. These are your bare essentials for living expenses only. I can assure you, once you know exactly what your minimum sales quota is to survive, you'll work toward that goal every week, and you'll hit the mark most of the time because you're focused. If you're a business owner, make this an assignment for your employees. When they get back to work on Monday, you'll see a big difference in their attitude.

You're Going to Get Lots of No's

In many businesses, the average close ratio is 10%. That means nine out of ten people will say no. Depending upon your type of product, it could be much higher. If you can't handle rejection on a daily basis, you're in the wrong business. Just realize they're rejecting your offer, not you.

You Must Believe in What You Sell

No matter how much knowledge you have about selling, none of it will do you any good if you don't have conviction in what you're selling. If you're working for a company that seems a little shady, you can NEVER attain success that way. Are you going to bed at night with a clear conscience? If not, you're holding your own success back.

Have Friends in Other Departments

In the real world of selling, it's a good idea to get along with people who work in different departments than yours. These people can make life miserable for you if you're constantly arguing with them. If you have a problem, go talk to them personally and ask them how you can make their job easier. The more you know how other departments work, the easier you can make their job.

Be Able to Let Go

Keep in mind, no single sale will make or break your selling career. Don't hang onto every prospect with the hopes they'll buy from you someday. Get them to make a decision. And if you must throw them away and move on, that's fine because it saves you time.

Expect Excellence

Tell yourself today, that anything in your selling career that's less than excellent is unacceptable. You will only function at one level: Superior.

Don't Be Penalized for Bad Service

If you've been in sales for a while, chances are you've had a few returns or chargebacks People do get buyers remorse and cancel. One thing you need to make sure of, is that you're not getting chargebacks from your company's poor customer service. Being a superstar salesperson means you're writing a lot of business and generating most of the income for your company. It's your responsibility to approach the owner or manager of the company you work for and get agreement that they will not penalize you for a chargeback due to poor customer service or an inferior product. No matter where or whom I work for, I always make sure that they understand this. Put it in writing and put it in your employee folder. If a customer has a problem and management takes weeks to get around to fixing it, the customer will more than likely cancel his order. This is not your fault and DO NOT TAKE THE BLAME FOR IT!

A company I once sold for gave me a $300 chargeback because of their poor customer service. I argued with them until I was blue in the face. To make my point, I took the week off. By me taking off, it cost the company more than $3,000 in lost revenue. They learned real quick that their poor customer service not only lost them a customer, but cost them thousands of dollars in lost revenue. I never ran into that problem again. Never, never, become a victim of chargebacks because of someone else's poor time management or lousy "don't care" attitude. Of course if they had buyers remorse, or you did a lousy job selling the person, then you have no one to blame but yourself if they cancel. I brought this up because superstars work and function at an entirely different level than most people would ever understand. Superstars can raise an entire company into a new way of thinking. Because of how much business they generate, the company sometimes has to hire other people to handle the work load. Your actions will motivate people to do better and improve themselves. Always remember this: being a superstar means the people around you have to perform at YOUR level. Never try to please people by going down to their level.

Breaking Out of a Slump

If you ever find yourself in a sales slump, often it's because you've gotten away from the basics. Go back to your script and stick to it for a week. Many times we forget some of the basics. Another good idea is to ask to train a new person. This forces you to go back to the absolute basics. Many companies know that by having a superstar train a new person, the superstar will have a fantastic week. I personally think superstars should train someone at least twice a year.

Listen to Tapes

To get your day started, instead of listening to music, listen to motivational tapes. It will get you primed and ready for the day. If you exercise in the morning, that's a good time to listen. You can also listen on your way to work.

Don't Sleep Away Your Success

I've never known any successful person who achieved success by sleeping late in the mornings. Train yourself to get up early, and get yourself ready for the day. Give yourself an hour of personal time in the morning, and you can achieve great things. Success is not for lazy people.

What is Your Mission?

Write yourself a mission statement. Have a creed you follow for your customers and your company.

Work for a Successful Company

Here's an interesting headline I read: "Poorly treated employees treat customers the same way." If you're an owner or manager, ask yourself, would you be a happy person working for your company as an employee? Do you have a high employee turnover rate? If so, your employees probably aren't happy working for you or your management. Running a boiler room operation screaming at people is the lowest level management style there is. These type of people are the dirt bags of the industry. Don't work for losers like that. They'll just drain your positive energy because they don't want anyone to succeed. You're better than that, move on to another company where your talents are appreciated. I did, and it was the best thing that I ever did for myself.

Don't Sell, Solve Problems

Think of your job as a problem solver. Top producers are good at solving customer's problems. Think out of the box and offer ideas and solutions from different angles. If you start doing that, the other person will automatically start the same process.

32

Motivational Quotes

"Without personal development, you have become all that you will ever be."
Eli Cohen

"The world belongs to the energetic."
Thomas Fuller

"Every accomplishment starts with the decision to try."
Anonymous

"Flaming enthusiasm, backed up by horse sense and persistence, is the quality that most frequently makes for success."
Dale Carnegie

"A man would do nothing if he waited until he could do it so well that no one could find fault."
John Henry Cardinal Newman

"Every morning, I get up and look through the Forbes list of the richest people in America. If I'm not there, I go to work."
Robert Orben

"Have the mental equipment to do your job, then take the job seriously, yourself not too seriously."
Frances Willis, U.S. Ambassador to Switzerland

"There is more credit and self-satisfaction in being a first-rate truck driver than a tenth-rate executive."
B.C. Forbes

"Problems are wake-up calls for creativity."
Gerhard Gschwandtner

"Only the bold get to the top."
Publilius Syrus

"Failures are divided into two classes; those who thought and never did, and those who did and never thought."
John Charles Salak

"Whoever admits he is too busy to improve his methods has acknowledged himself to be at the end of his rope."
J. Ogden Armour

"Give everybody a chance to buy. Rather than determining without an interview that some people will not buy, take it for granted that everybody can buy."
John Henry Patterson

"Our greatest weakness lies in giving up. The most certain way to succeed is to always try just one more time."
Thomas A. Edison

"Sales managers without standards for persistence teach salespeople to follow the line of least resistance."

Gerhard Gschwandtner

"To please people is a great step towards persuading them."

Lord Chesterfield

"It is not the quantity, but the pertinence of your words that does the business."

Seneca

"Great successes never come without risks."

Flavius

"Practice is just as valuable as a sale. The sale will make you a living; the skill will make you a fortune."

Jim Rohn

"Winning starts with beginning."

Robert H. Schuller

"Nothing focuses the mind better than the constant sight of a competitor who wants to wipe you off the map."

Wayne Calloway

"A competitor is the guy who goes in a revolving door behind you and comes out ahead of you."

George Romney

"Timely service, like timely gifts, is doubled in value."

George MacDonald

"From the errors of others, a wise man corrects his own."

Syrus

"If you have a job without aggravations, you don't have a job."

Malcolm Forbes

"One of the biggest factors in success is the courage to undertake something."

James A. Worsham

"To exist is to change, to change is to mature, to mature is to go on creating oneself endlessly."

Henri Bergson

"I have accepted fear as a part of life, specifically the fear of change, I have gone ahead despite the pounding in the heart that says: turn back."

Erica Jong

"Sweat is the cologne of accomplishment."

Arthur Jones

"If you're going to be thinking you might as well think big."

Donald Trump

"Success comes from good judgment. Good judgment comes from experience. Experience comes from bad judgment."

Arthur Jones

"The key to success is never to follow the others."
Masaru Ibuka

"Not failure, but low aim, is a crime."
James Russell Lowell

"The great man is the man who does a thing for the first time."
Alexander Smith

"He was a "how" thinker, not an "if" thinker."
Unknown

"To win you have to risk loss."
Jean-Claude Killy

"If there is no wind, row."
Latin proverb

"Imagination is one of the last remaining legal means you have to gain an unfair advantage over your competition."
Pat Fallon

33

Mandatory Reading List

In sales, a lot of people have experience, but they don't have an understanding of the selling process. That's one of the reasons I feel that ongoing learning is essential. Here are just some of the books I feel should be part of any successful salesperson's library. I could have listed 100 books, but felt this would be a good start for you. Get ready for a major education. Good luck and success.

(Note: To find these books, you can simply type in the title at amazon.com or barnesandnoble.com, or give the ISBN number to the clerk at your local book store.)

"Spin Selling" (field book) by Neil Rackham ISBN 0-07-052235-9 paperback. One of the best books ever written on selling. It's a course that teaches you how to ask questions and take people through the sales cycle. There are several *"Spin Selling"* books, but you want the field book. This book changed my entire way of thinking about sales. If I had one book on sales, this would be it.

"Prospecting Your Way To Sales Success," by Bill Good ISBN 0-684-84203-3. Hard cover (updated version). This is the same method I personally use. It shows you old school techniques versus new school. It's about getting in and out of calls quickly and finding a buyer, Today!

"How To Sell More In Less Time With No Rejection, Volume 2," by Art Sobczak. ISBN 1-881081-07-9 .Paperback. Art's one of the best in the business. I've been to his Telesales Rep College course and have been using his techniques for years. You can visit his web site at: BusinessByPhone. com. You can sign up for a free weekly newsletter on selling tips. I highly recommend his monthly newsletter, *"The Telephone Selling Report."* Tell him I referred you to him.

"Advanced Selling Strategies," by Brian Tracy ISBN 0-671-86519-6 Hardback & Paperback. This book is for people who have to go out on appointments. It takes you through the sales process. Many of the principles can be applied to phone sales. Brian has been around for years and is considered one of the most respected in the industry. It's well written and easy to understand.

"Guerilla Marketing (Weapons)," by Jay Conrad Levinson. ISBN 0-452-26519-3. Paperback. This book is filled with 100 ways to market yourself or company. Many of them are free or very inexpensive. Jay has been around for years and is considered one of the modern marketing gurus. He has an entire guerilla marketing series, but you want the (weapons) book. It's excellent for small business owners on a shoe string budget.

"The Call Center Resource Catalog." Phone 1-800-243-6002. Ask for the educational catalog. This catalog will put you right in the vein of the telemarketing industry. It has books, magazines, tapes, etc. You'll find everything you're looking for here. The catalog's free. I can personally vouch for their books. They're well written and simple to read. If you see something you'd like to have, order it. You won't be disappointed.

"Secrets Of Closing Sales," by Charles Roth & Roy Alexander. ISBN 0-13-671512-5. Paperback. I personally like this book a lot. It's so direct and simple. The premise is to make sure your entire approach is based on closing. It really shows you how to ask for the order as soon as you hear signals. Whether face to face, or on the phone, you'll become a much stronger closer after reading this.

"E-mail El Dorado," by Dr. Jeffrey Lant. ISBN 0-940374-38-2. Phone 617-547-6372. Paperback. Not getting the results from your web site you thought you would? This book is light years ahead of its time. Jeffrey really shows you the key to making big money on the net. No matter what product or service you sell, this is for you. The concept is based on collecting people's e-mail addresses, and using them to your advantage without spamming. If you're serious about making money on the net, order this book.

"Dealing With People You Can't Stand," by Dr. Rick Brinkman & Dr. Rick Kirschner, ISBN 0-07-007838-6. Paperback. This book is exactly what it says it is. You might wonder why I put this in as a book to read. The bottom line is that we all work or have customers that are extremely difficult to work with. This book explains the 10 different personality types in a fun and humorous way. I personally use this approach and can tell you it works like a charm.

"New Strategic Selling by Stephen Heiman & Diane Sanchez" ISBN 0-446-67346-3. Paperback. This book is for people who sell big ticket items to large corporations. This book is very advanced and explains how people at different positions in major corporations have to be sold differently at each level. It identifies the four real decision makers in a corporate labyrinth. It's a very interesting read but may not be for everyone. It's really for those high level corporate sales. People who sell to major franchises, or big name Fortune 500 companies would benefit from this.

www. amazon. com. The best bookstore on the net. Go to their site and type in telemarketing. It will literally bring up hundreds of books. Be sure to check the date of when the book was published. You don't want to order something that was written in 1947. This will really give you a good idea of the type of information that's out there.

"1001 Ways To Reward Employees," by Bob Nelson ISBN 1-56305-339-X. Paperback. This is a book for managers who want to keep their sales force motivated with fun contests. As we all know, the top producers always win. This book makes things fair for everyone.

"The Vocal Advantage," by Jeffrey Jacobi. ISBN 0-13-103664-5. Paperback with cassette. An excellent course on improving your speech. This is a must read for anyone who speaks with people face to face or over the phone.

The *"Mind Map Book,"* by Tony Buzan. ISBN 0-452-27322-6. Paperback. How to use radiant thinking to maximize your brain's untapped potential. If this method of learning was used in our educational system, there would be very few people failing. I use his methods every day.

"Success is a Choice," by Rick Pitino. ISBN 076790-1320. If you're a manager, you need to understand that you're running a team. If you're an individual, it will let you know if you deserve to be successful. This is a good read, and very motivating.

Conclusion

I guess by now you realize that just picking up the phone and blabbing away will get you nowhere fast. There's an exact science and art to becoming a pro on the phone. It takes hard work and dedication. The phone's the lifeline to your livelihood. You use it just about everyday of your life. You need to have phone awareness. That's having a full understanding of what you're saying and what you're trying to achieve.

Contrary to popular belief, dialing is not a numbers game. If that was the case, then everyone would make the same amount of money. Top producers do things differently. They really have an acute awareness of the selling process. You need to have a presence of mind that it's a war out there.

Sales is not for lazy people. Start making it a point to think of your phone as the most important part of your marketing strategy. It doesn't matter how much you spend on advertising. If you can't make the sale or set the appointment when people call you, you're just wasting your money.

You've learned a ton of selling techniques and concepts, now go back and slowly start incorporating them into your selling strategy. Don't be afraid to mold or bend the ideas to fit your particular situation. Don't be afraid of change. Be creative and follow through. Keep things simple. What works for you, keep, what doesn't, get rid of. Always be looking for that better idea or concept.

If you're a manager or business owner you can take some of the exercises out of the book and have everyone get involved. Make it a game. For example, have everyone list all the reasons why someone should use your product or service, then go over them with everyone in the office. If you have a special idea or technique you use, let me know about it. Now go find one idea you highlighted and start practicing it tomorrow. Keep in mind, not every technique works every single time. They're designed to put the numbers on your side. **NOW GET ON THE PHONE AND MAKE SOME MONEY!**

Joe Catal "Saleman"

P.S. Thanks to my wonderful wife for all those 4 and 5 a.m. breakfasts she made for me while I was up at the crack of dawn working on this project. I also want to thank her for those lonely dinners she had while I wrote into the night. She's really been a good sport about the whole thing. I'm very fortunate to be in love with such a wonderful woman.

Special Services

Customized Script Development

I will personally write and design scripts for you. Opening statements, voice mail/answering machine, call backs, etc. Prices vary depending on your personal needs. It's very affordable if you're a millionaire.

E-mail me at: saleman@bellsouth.net

-Notes-

-Notes-

-Notes-

-Notes-

Here Are Other Resources You Can Get Right Now to Help You Close More Sales Using The Phone!

FREE! The Telesales Hot Tip of the Week Email Newsletter

Each week you'll receive a new issue containing several telesales tips you can use right now. Sign up, and see free back issues at

www.BusinessByPhone.com

Get a FREE Subscription to the Business By Phone Catalog of Tapes, Books, Telesales Rep College Seminars, Other Training Materials

If you use the phone in any aspect of sales or service, you'll find something in this catalog to help you do it better. Also, especially if you didn't buy this book through us, you'll want to be listed in our database so you can be one of the first to be notified of new books and resources to help you sell more by phone. Call our offices at 1-800-326-7721 or (402)895-9399.

The Telesales Rep College Two-Day Training Workshops

Throughout the year we hold 8-10 public training programs across the U.S., covering every step of the professional telesales call. Valuable for rookies and veterans alike, you'll leave energized, armed with new ideas to deploy right away to grab more business on your very next call. Only 25 participants accepted per session. Call 1-800-326-7721, (402)895-9399, or go to www.BusinessByPhone.com for a schedule.

Sales-Building Materials You Can Order Right Now

The "Telephone Selling Report" Sales Tips Newsletter

If you enjoyed this book, get more of this same type of sales-building material delivered to your desk every month in the eight-page *"Telephone Selling Report."* $69 for a one-year, six-issue, subscription.

"How to Sell More, In Less Time, With No Rejection, Using Common Sense Telephone Techniques—Volumes 1and 2"
By Art Sobczak

A fine complement to the book you're now holding, and a must-have for successful sales pros. In these two books, you get over 540 pages of solid tips. Art Sobczak details instantly-usable ideas on all parts of the sales call. If you liked this book, and are looking for additional ideas with the same consultative philosophy of sales, you'll find it here. The title of the book says it all. Guaranteed! **$59.00 (+$6 shipping).**

To Order Any of These Items

1. Mail your check, U.S. funds only, to Business By Phone, 13254 Stevens St., Omaha, NE, 68137.

2. Go to www.BusinessByPhone.com

3. Call us at 1-800-326-7721, or (402)895-9399.

4. Fax your order with credit card number to (402)896-3353. *(Overseas shipping billed at cost. Candian shipping 2x listed rate.)*

To Get More Copies of This Book:

To get additional copies of this book, photocopy or remove this form, or call or fax us with the necessary information. *(Inquire about quantity discounts. Also, bookstore and dealer inquiries welcome.)*

Yes, please send me _____ copies of *"Telesales Tips from the Trenches,"* at $19.50 (U.S. funds) each (+$3.50 shipping in the U.S., $7 Canada, overseas charged at cost.)

Name_____

Company_____

Address_____

City_____State_____Zip Code_____

Phone_____

Fax_____._____

Method of Payment

☐Visa/MC/AMEX/Discover

#_____

sig._____exp._____

☐ Check /Money Order Enclosed *(U.S. Funds Only)*

Ways to Order

• **Phone** your order to **1-800-326-7721**, or (402)895-9399.

• **Fax** your order to (402)896-3353.

• **Mail** your order to Business By Phone, 13254-B1 Stevens St., Omaha, NE, 68137.

• **E-Mail** your order to **orders@businessbyphone.com**